Chemical and
Biological Warfare

Other Books in the Global Viewpoints Series

GLOBAL VIEWPOINTS

Chemical and Biological Warfare

Lisa Idzikowski, Book Editor

GREENHAVEN
PUBLISHING

Published in 2020 by Greenhaven Publishing, LLC
353 3rd Avenue, Suite 255, New York, NY 10010

Articles in Greenhaven Publishing anthologies are often edited for length to meet page
requirements. In addition, original titles of these works are changed to clearly present
the main thesis and to explicitly indicate the author's opinion. Every effort is made to
ensure that Greenhaven Publishing accurately reflects the original intent of the authors.
Every effort has been made to trace the owners of the copyrighted material.

Cover image: Peter Turnley/Corbis/VCG via Getty Images
Map: frees/Shutterstock.com

Library of Congress Cataloging-in-Publication Data

Names: Idzikowski, Lisa, editor.
Title: Chemical and biological warfare / Lisa Idzikowski, book editor.
Description: First edition. | New York : Greenhaven Publishing, [2020] |
  Series: Global viewpoints | Includes bibliographical references and index. | Audience:
  Grades 9-12.
Identifiers: LCCN 2018060287| ISBN 9781534505483 (library bound) | ISBN
  9781534505490 (pbk.)
Subjects: LCSH: Chemical warfare. | Biological warfare. | Chemical
  warfare—Moral and ethical aspects. | Biological warfare—Moral and
  ethical aspects. | Chemical warfare—Government policy. | Biological
  warfare—Government policy.
Classification: LCC UG447 .C5155 2020 | DDC 358/.34—dc23
LC record available at https://lccn.loc.gov/2018060287

Manufactured in the United States of America

Website: http://greenhavenpublishing.com

Contents

Chapter 2: The Effects of Chemical and Biological Warfare

Chapter 3: Why Do Terrorists Use Chemical and Biological Weapons?

Chapter 4: The Future of Chemical and Biological Warfare

Foreword

> *"The problems of all of humanity can*
> *only be solved by all of humanity."*
> *—Swiss author Friedrich Dürrenmatt*

Global interdependence has become an undeniable reality. Mass media and technology have increased worldwide access to information and created a society of global citizens. Understanding and navigating this global community is a challenge, requiring a high degree of information literacy and a new level of learning sophistication.

Building on the success of its flagship series, Opposing Viewpoints, Greenhaven Publishing has created the Global Viewpoints series to examine a broad range of current, often controversial topics of worldwide importance from a variety of international perspectives. Providing students and other readers with the information they need to explore global connections and think critically about worldwide implications, each Global Viewpoints volume offers a panoramic view of a topic of widespread significance.

Drugs, famine, immigration—a broad, international treatment is essential to do justice to social, environmental, health, and political issues such as these. Junior high, high school, and early college students, as well as general readers, can all use Global Viewpoints anthologies to discern the complexities relating to each issue. Readers will be able to examine unique national perspectives while, at the same time, appreciating the interconnectedness that global priorities bring to all nations and cultures.

Material in each volume is selected from a diverse range of sources, including journals, magazines, newspapers, nonfiction books, speeches, government documents, pamphlets, organization newsletters, and position papers. Global Viewpoints is truly global, with material drawn primarily from international sources available in English and secondarily from US sources with extensive international coverage.

Features of each volume in the Global Viewpoints series include:

- An **annotated table of contents** that provides a brief summary of each essay in the volume, including the name of the country or area covered in the essay.

- An **introduction** specific to the volume topic.

- A **world map** to help readers locate the countries or areas covered in the essays.

- For each viewpoint, an **introduction** that contains notes about the author and source of the viewpoint explains why material from the specific country is being presented, summarizes the main points of the viewpoint, and offers three **guided reading questions** to aid in understanding and comprehension.

- **For further discussion questions** that promote critical thinking by asking the reader to compare and contrast aspects of the viewpoints or draw conclusions about perspectives and arguments.

- A worldwide list of **organizations to contact** for readers seeking additional information.

- A **periodical bibliography** for each chapter and a **bibliography of books** on the volume topic to aid in further research.

- A comprehensive **subject index** to offer access to people, places, events, and subjects cited in the text.

Global Viewpoints is designed for a broad spectrum of readers who want to learn more about current events, history, political science, government, international relations, economics, environmental science, world cultures, and sociology—students doing research for class assignments or debates, teachers and faculty seeking to supplement course materials, and others wanting to understand current issues better. By presenting how people in various countries perceive the root causes, current consequences, and proposed solutions to worldwide challenges, Global Viewpoints volumes offer readers opportunities to enhance their global awareness and their knowledge of cultures worldwide.

Introduction

> *"Five years ago, the Assad regime launched missiles containing a cocktail of deadly gas at the people of Ghouta. One thousand, four hundred, twenty-nine people were killed. On April 4, 2017, the Assad regime dropped sarin gas from the sky on the people of Khan Sheikhoun. The attack killed over 70 innocent Syrians—including dozens of children ... Then, in April 2018, over 40 people died, and hundreds received treatment for exposure to chemical weapons in Douma."*
> —Ambassador Nikki Haley, US Representative to the United Nations, September 6, 2018.

The United States Department of Homeland Security, an arm of the US federal government, aims to protect the United States from all types of threats. The agency is concerned that America is facing an increasing danger of attack by weapons of mass destruction from terrorists and rogue states. According to the agency, "a weapon of mass destruction is a nuclear, radiological, chemical, biological, or other device that is intended to harm a large number of people." Chemical and biological weapons fall into this category as defined by Homeland Security.

Terrorism is nothing new. Its practitioners have used many forms of weaponry throughout history, including chemical and biological. Long ago Mongols used an early form of biological weapon by launching plague infested corpses in attacks against their enemies. During World War II the United States dropped atomic bombs over the Japanese cities of Hiroshima and Nagasaki. More recently, news reports have been filled with various accounts of the proliferation, detection, destruction, and use of chemical and biological weapons. It's not surprising that according to the Roper Center for Public Opinion Research, as recently as 2014, 23 percent of Americans fear that a deadly virus of some type will cause death, destruction, and an end to humanity.

People around the globe have seen the effects of chemical weapons on human beings. Photos and videos from inside Syria in April of 2018 appear to show victims suffering the effects of chemical weapons attack. Patients flooding into area hospitals showed signs that may indicate they suffered from exposure to chemicals. According to the Syrian American Medical Society, patients displayed various symptoms of "respiratory distress, central cyanosis, excessive oral foaming, corneal burns and the emission of chlorine-like odor." This modern-day evidence of chemical exposure parallels accounts from history which recorded the effects on soldiers and civilians suffering from the chemical weapons used during World War I.

The negative effects of toxic weapons are undeniable. But do they offer any possible positive value? Biological research has often provided valuable insight for medical treatments—some accidental such as the discovery of penicillin—or purposeful as in the discovery and development of certain drugs used to treat different forms of cancer. "Dual-use" research refers to scientific findings that could be used for the good of humankind or—if acquired by potential evil-doers—could become formulated into horrific weapons. Research from 2011 into the influenza virus demonstrates this double-edged sword. The original research findings were intended to help medical clinicians fight or treat the disease. On the flip side, some worried that by publishing the information in scientific journals it could essentially provide a recipe for the malicious formation of virulent strains of virus which might become biological weapons used by terrorists.

The global community is anxious about the potential use of chemical and biological weapons. Countries have worked together towards preventive strategies, signing treaties against the use of these dangerous substances. But international laws have not been enough to deter action by some countries. Because Syria has ignored diplomatic pressure to stop its use of chemical weapons, it suffered military reprisals in the spring of 2018. Combined forces from France, the United Kingdom, and the United States launched airstrikes aimed at destroying chemical research sites and storage facilities. France's president, Emmanuel Macron, released a statement saying "we cannot tolerate the recurring use of chemical weapons, which is an immediate danger for the Syrian people and our collective security." British Prime Minister Theresa May concluded it was time for action because "we have sought to use every possible diplomatic channel to achieve this. But our efforts have been repeatedly thwarted." And US Defense Secretary James Mattis declared "together we have sent a clear message: ... Syrian President Bashar al-Assad ... should not perpetrate another chemical weapons attack."

There is absolutely no doubt that chemical and biological weapons are a worrisome subject for humankind. The international community must continue to work together to prevent the use of these weapons of mass destruction before it is too late. Shedding light on this challenging topic—its possible causes, global interest, and preventive measures—in this volume, the authors represented in *Global Viewpoints: Chemical and Biological Warfare* offer a diverse array of global perspectives.

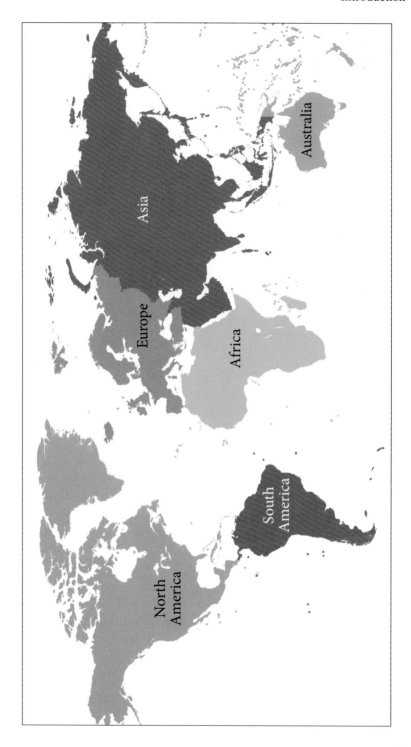

CHAPTER 1

Chemical and Biological Weapons Around the World

In Syria Chemical Weapons Are in Use

Cindy Vestergaard

In the following viewpoint, Cindy Vestergaard argues that Syria is using deadly chemical weapons and provides evidence cited by the World Health Organization as proof. The author elaborates on the US justification for airstrikes that occurred as a result, muddying the waters with confusion as to whether or not the US played into the hands of Syrian leader Bashar al-Assad. Finally, the author outlines Russia's underwhelming response. Vestergaard is a senior associate at the Stimson Center, specializing in nuclear safeguards.

As you read, consider the following questions:

1. According to the author, why did the World Health Organization believe that chemical weapons were used?
2. As defined in the viewpoint, what are barrel bombs?
3. Does Russia agree with the US according to Vestergaard?

I mages from the attack on Khan Sheikhoun on April 4 showed victims limp, with pinpoint eyes and frothing mouths, as emergency responders rushed to strip clothes from bodies and hose away chemical substances. For many, the US strikes on a Syrian air base two days later were a satisfying response and long overdue in a protracted, deadly civil war that has left millions of families shattered, Daesh emboldened and Assad seemingly immune.

"Deterrence Isn't Enough to Keep Syria from Using Chemical Weapons," by Cindy Vestergaard, April 19, 2017. Reprinted by permission

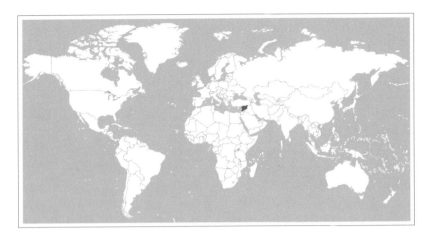

The following day, the World Health Organization issued a statement that symptoms, including the lack of visible external injuries, were consistent with exposure to nerve agents. Some of the victims sent to Turkey for treatment, who later died, reportedly tested positive for sarin. Taken together with conclusions by the Joint Investigative Mechanism (JIM) that Syrian forces deployed chlorine as a weapon on at least three occasions in the northern province of Idlib in 2014 and 2015, a number of capitals, including Washington, concluded that Assad was responsible for the attacks. The Trump administration claimed that it struck Shayrat Air Base, from which it said the attack on April 4 had been launched.

After the attacks on Khan Sheikhoun, the Organisation for the Prohibition of Chemical Weapons (OPCW) issued a statement that it had already begun collecting and analyzing data. Its investigations and conclusions provide vital independent, third-party evidence on violations of the Chemical Weapons Convention, for the international community to decide upon action. Accordingly, there is concern that the strikes ordered by Trump were too hasty—that time for the OPCW and the JIM is needed to investigate and confirm sarin use, and identify who is responsible, before military action is taken.

The need for investigation is underscored by previous sarin attacks in Syria. Inquiries confirmed the attacks at Ghouta back in August 2013 released sarin on a relatively large scale, but the perpetrators have never been formally identified. There is convincing evidence that surface-to-surface rockets were used, which the Syrian military, not the opposition, were believed to possess. However, the UN Security Council excluded the Ghouta attacks from the JIM's mandate, limiting its scope only to investigating allegations that the OPCW has confirmed involved chemical agents since 2014. Moreover, an OPCW report from last August detailed discoveries of precursors for agents like soman and VX at several undeclared facilities in Syria. In other words, while the OPCW has verified that all of Syria's declared chemical weapons have been destroyed, it has not been able to confirm the entire program has been eliminated.

The US strikes are likely a one-off, sending a "message" that the use of chemical weapons will no longer be tolerated, although the messaging required further clarification and explanation. White House press secretary Sean Spicer said last week that the administration would respond in a similar fashion "if you gas a baby or if you put a barrel bombing to innocent people." Spicer had to later clarify that if the barrel bombs—a weapon routinely used by Syrian forces—contained chemical agents, then a military response would be possible. President Trump stated that the United States would not get involved with Syria, but would continue attacks if the use of chemical weapons is repeated. As the messaging is being refined, the Trump policy seems to be one of counterproliferation.

In their Final Communiqué on April 10–11, G-7 leaders stated that US action against the Shayrat airfield "was a carefully calibrated, limited in scope response" to the attacks at Khan Sheikhoun "in order to prevent and deter the proliferation and use of deadly chemical weapons in Syria." After the meeting, US secretary of state Rex Tillerson stated the US strikes were a matter of national security: "We do not want the regime's uncontrolled stockpile of chemical weapons to fall into the hands of ISIS, or other terrorist groups and want to attack the United States and our allies."

In the lead-up to his meeting with Russian foreign minister Sergey Lavrov, Tillerson pointed fingers at Russia for failing in its responsibility to uphold numerous UN Security Council resolutions on Syria's chemical-weapons program. He stated that it was "unclear whether Russia failed to take its obligation seriously or Russia has been incompetent." Meanwhile, Russia is digging in with its support for Assad, claiming opponents and rebels were responsible for "false flag" chemical-weapon attacks as a means to draw in the United States into the Syrian conflict. Putin recently stated that Russia has information that more of these attacks are planned to blame the Assad regime as a pretext for further military action.

As the first bilateral meetings between American and Russian ministers of foreign affairs proceeded against the Syrian backdrop, the Trump administration became more consistent in its messaging that it is willing to use force to counter the proliferation and use of chemical weapons. The decision to pull the USS Carl Vinson from planned naval military exercises in Australia and send it towards the Korean Peninsula suggested that the administration's messaging may include using force to counter the proliferation of nuclear weapons. Using counterproliferation to guide foreign policy is a familiar one. As noted by Aaron Blake, the Trump Doctrine is sounding suspiciously like the Bush Doctrine.

A policy based primarily on counterproliferation is challenged by its limited use of diplomacy. There may be a consensus that counterproliferation is a tool to provide teeth to nonproliferation, but without a true desire for diplomatic solutions, both sides will fail to uphold the UN resolutions negotiated and passed to hold those accountable.

In the United States Bioterrorism Is a Threat

Jack Spenser and Michael Scardaville

In the following viewpoint, written just after the September 11 terrorist attacks, Jack Spenser and Michael Scardaville argue that the United States is vulnerable to terrorist attacks using biological agents as weapons. The authors analyze possible biological agents, their effectiveness against people, countries actively pursuing biological weapons, and whether the US is prepared for a bioterrorism attack. Spenser is the Vice President for the Institute for Economic Freedom and oversees research at The Heritage Foundation. Scardaville is a former political analyst.

As you read, consider the following questions:

1. According to the authors, what are three possible targets for terrorists to use against America?
2. As stated by the authors, what are two possible biological agents used for bioterrorism?
3. What US government agency is tasked with dealing with the threat of bioterrorism according to the viewpoint?

The September 11 terrorist attacks on the World Trade Center and the Pentagon made starkly clear how vulnerable Americans are to terrorism at home. But as devastating as those attacks were, the likelihood is growing that terrorists may soon

"Understanding the Bioterrorist Threat: Facts and Figures," by Jack Spencer and Michael Scardaville, The Heritage Foundation, October 11, 2001. Reprinted by permission.

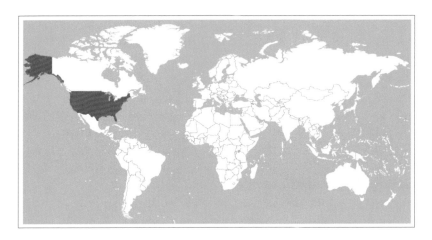

decide to use biological agents as weapons to extract even higher death tolls. Evidence of this includes the startling fact that the number of criminal investigations in the United States related to the use of biological materials as weapons of mass destruction more than doubled between 1997 and 1998:

- In 1997, 22 of the 74 criminal investigations—or 30 percent—involved biological materials.
- In 1998, 112 of the 181 criminal investigations—or 62 percent—involved biological materials.

As the facts about possible biological agents and the figures about their potential effects become known, the challenges for terrorists in mounting a biological attack against America may appear daunting, but they are not impossible to meet. Biological warfare is neither new nor theoretical; it has been waged effectively, in fact, since the 14th century.

The most likely targets for bioterrorist attacks on America are people, crops, and livestock. Moreover, some of the agents are relatively easy to obtain: In 1996, an Ohio man was able to purchase bubonic plague cultures through the mail. And there are various means of delivery. Biological agents can be spread by airborne release; by injection or direct contact; through food, pharmaceutical, and water contamination; or by animal vectors such as fleas and hair. And as recent simulated exercises in various US cities have shown, the United States is still ill-prepared to respond to such attacks.

According to the Centers for Disease Control and Prevention (CDC), biological agents pose a risk to national security because they are easily disseminated; cause high mortality, which would have a major impact on public health systems; cause panic and social disruptions; and require special action and funding to increase public preparedness. As the following facts and figures show, the challenges facing the Bush Administration, the new Office of Homeland Security, and Congress in responding to the growing threat of bioterrorism are immense.

The Use of Biological Weapons

Biological weapons can be produced from widely available pathogens that are manufactured for legitimate biomedical research or obtained from soil or infected animals and humans. In fact, many of the infectious diseases that are associated with biological warfare are endemic to the same countries that are most often suspected of trying to develop biological weapons. And because biological agents may be cheap and easy to obtain, any nation with a basic industry or facility such as a brewery has a de facto capability to produce biological weapons.

Past Bioterrorist Attacks

Since 1346, when the Mongols catapulted corpses contaminated with plague over the walls into Kaffa (Crimea) and forced the besieged Genoans to flee, there have been many documented cases of the use of biological agents against people.

- In 1767, during the French and Indian Wars, the British gave hostile Indians the blankets they had used to wrap British smallpox victims. The disease quickly spread among the Indians.

- During World War I, the Germans used glanders and other microbial agents to infect draft animals herded into ports within the United States and Argentina en route to the western front.

- From 1932 to 1945, Japanese forces in Manchuria experimented with plague-infected fleas, anthrax, cholera, and several other diseases to use as biological weapons. Japan conducted field trials against Chinese cities in the late 1930s. The agents were sprayed from aircraft and placed in water or food supplies, with mixed results. There were several plague outbreaks in Chinese cities. Japan reportedly has killed 1,700 of its own troops through mishaps in developing biological weapons.

- The Bulgarian secret police are known for developing a means to assassinate someone by shooting a pellet enriched with ricin, a highly lethal toxin cultivated from a poisonous protein in the castor bean, from the tip of an umbrella into the victim's skin. In September 1978, the Bulgarian secret police used this method to assassinate dissident Georgi Markov in London.

- In 1979, a plume of anthrax released in Sverdlovsk, Russia, killed 66 of 77 reported infected people who were downwind from the release point. Livestock 10 to 100 kilometers downwind also died. In 1992, President Boris Yeltsin admitted that the tragedy was due to an accident at a former Soviet biological weapons facility.

- In 1984 in Oregon, the Rajneeshee religious cult contaminated salad bars in local restaurants with salmonella bacteria in an effort to prevent people from voting in a local election. Although no one died, 751 people were diagnosed with the food-borne illness.

- In 1986, Tamil guerrillas operating in Sri Lanka poisoned tea with potassium cyanide in an effort to cripple the Sri Lankan tea export industry.

- In 1993, Iran reportedly plotted to contaminate water supplies in the United States and Europe with an unspecified biological agent, and Israeli Arabs plotted to poison the water in Galilee with an "unidentified powder."

- In 1994, the Aum Shinrikyo cult attempted to release anthrax from the tops of buildings in Tokyo. In 1995, the cult placed three briefcases designed to spray botulinum toxin in the Tokyo subway in an attack that ultimately failed.

- In 1995, two members of a Minnesota militia, the Patriots Council, were convicted of possessing ricin that they planned to use against law-enforcement officers who had served legal papers on members of the group.

Clearly, the threat of biological terrorism is real and growing.

Possible Biological Agents
The menu of biological agents that could inflict massive harm on Americans is broad. The viruses, bacteria, or other toxins can be relatively easy to acquire, process, and disseminate or very difficult and unstable, with many possibilities between those extremes. The likelihood that a terrorist will use one agent over another depends on these factors as well as on how lethal the agent is and whether there is a vaccine or treatment readily available to counter its effects.

Anthrax. The focus on anthrax as a possible biological weapon for a terrorist attack grew significantly following the recent death from anthrax of a man in Florida and the discovery that his coworker has anthrax spores in his nostrils. Anthrax infections can occur either from inhalation of the spores or from skin contact. Inhalation anthrax is almost always fatal once the symptoms—which mimic influenza—appear.

The anthrax bacterium (Bacillus anthracis) is most prevalent in agricultural regions, where the spore occurs naturally among animals. These regions include South and Central America, Southern and Eastern Europe, Asia, Africa, the Caribbean, and the Middle East. Outbreaks occur in both wild and domestic cattle, sheep, goats, camels, antelopes, and other herbivores, but they can also occur in humans who have been exposed to infected animals or to tissue from infected animals.

Additional facts affecting its possible use by terrorists include the following:

- Anthrax can be cultured from almost any soil that supports livestock. Anthrax seed stock, however, is difficult to process and disseminate with great success. The minimal lethal dose for inhalation of anthrax (reportedly 5,000 to 10,000 spores) is high compared with other biological agents.

- Most infections (about 95 percent) occur when the bacterium enters a cut or skin abrasion—for example, in unprotected workers handling the wool, hides, leather, or hair products (especially goat hair) of infected animals. Skin infection begins as an itchy bump resembling an insect bite; within two days, it develops into a vesicle and then a painless ulcer, usually 1–3 cm in diameter, with a characteristic black necrotic (dying) area in the center. Lymph glands in the area may swell. About 20 percent of untreated cases of infection through the skin result in death. Deaths are rare with appropriate antimicrobial therapy.

- The anthrax vaccine is effective for preventing anthrax infection through the skin. It appears to be effective for some, but not all, strains of inhalation anthrax in some animal species. Testing to determine the effectiveness and possible side effects of this vaccine is ongoing.

Smallpox. Smallpox is also mentioned frequently as a possible biological weapon. The reasons: The disease is highly infectious and associated with a high mortality rate. Little vaccine is available, and there is no effective treatment for the disease.

Currently, no one under the age of 30 has been vaccinated against smallpox. For physicians, the most difficult aspect of diagnosing the disease is a lack of familiarity with it.

In 1980, the World Health Organization (WHO) declared endemic smallpox eradicated, with the last occurrence in Somalia in 1977. Currently, there are only two WHO-approved and inspected repositories: the Centers for Disease Control and Prevention (CDC) in the United States and Vector Laboratories in Russia. However, clandestine stockpiles may exist.

Potential Means of Delivery

Biological agents can be spread by aerosol sprays, explosives, or the contamination of food or water supplies. The effectiveness of an attack can be affected by the particle size of the agent itself, the stability of the agent under desiccating conditions, exposure to ultraviolet light, wind speed and direction, and atmospheric stability.

In most terrorist incidents that involved chemical or biological contamination, the method of dissemination is unknown. In cases where the method has been identified, the terrorists have relied on airborne dissemination (17 percent); pharmaceutical contamination (16 percent); food or drink contamination (15 percent); injection or direct contact (13 percent); and water contamination (11 percent).

Additional facts regarding delivery of biological weapons that counterterrorism planners must consider include the following:

- No reliable fixed means exist for detecting biological agents released into the atmosphere over large areas such as cities. Biological attacks are likely to be recognized only after affected people start to become sick. In some cases, this may not occur for weeks after an attack.

- There are various plausible scenarios for biological and chemical contamination of agricultural products (similar, for example, to the German practice in World War I). These include infecting livestock with hoof and mouth disease, pigs with African Swine Fever, chicken with the

Newcastle disease virus, or crops (such as wheat, corn, rice, or soy beans) with Karnal Bunt, stem rust, or leaf rust.

- Imported materials could be used by terrorists to introduce pathogens into a country. These include straw, animal feed, and fertilizer. Imports infected before they leave the country of origin could facilitate multiple outbreaks over large geographic areas in recipient countries, mimicking a natural event (such as the recent outbreak of hoof and mouth disease in Japanese cattle in two widely separated areas).

- The greatest number of potential casualties involves the airborne release of biological and chemical agents. Releases within enclosed spaces (such as subways, buildings, domed sports arenas, airports, or train stations) require less of these agents but are likely to be quite lethal because the agent remains concentrated in the confined airspace. Such releases would require less than about 1 gram of biological agents.

- Open-air release of biological and chemical weapons can affect the broadest area with the highest number of casualties. Temperature inversions, in particular, could trap these agents close to the ground, substantially increasing the level of surface doses. Rain washes most of these agents out of the air. Some biological and chemical agents may remain harmful in groundwater for a period of time; however, most become harmless.

- Biological agents may be aerosolized by explosion or by use of a spray nozzle. Explosive release tends to be inefficient (according to one estimate, leaving approximately 0.1 percent to 1 percent of the agents in the 1 to 5 micron size range), with the heat and shock of the explosion destroying much of the agent. Spray release is more efficient (up to 25 percent efficient for liquid slurries and up to 40 percent for dry biological agents that are ground to the proper size before dispersal).

Nations That Threatened the World

The weapons of mass destruction (WMD) come in three forms, nuclear weapons, biological weapons including toxins, and chemical weapons. Three global treaties prohibit the development and production of the WMD: Nuclear Non-Proliferation Treaty (NPT, 1970), Biological Weapons Convention (BWC, 1975), and Chemical Weapons Convention (CWC, 1977). The 1970s was a valuable decade for beginning the process of eliminating the WMD. Over the years, some nations have been reluctant to ratify the WMD treaties.

As of May 1, 2017, out of a total of 195 nation-states in the world, 191 are parties to the NPT, 178 are parties to the BWC, and 192 are parties to the CWC. The BWC is the least subscribed WMD treaty and efforts are underway to bring more nations into its prohibitive orbit.

Ratification and accession bind a nation-state to the fullest extent under a treaty whereas mere signing a treaty imposes some obligations not to defeat the object and purpose of the treaty. International law does not require the two-step process of signing and ratifying treaties. Nations may directly ratify (called accession) a treaty without first signing it. For example, China ratified the BWC in 1984 without first signing it. Here I use the word ratification to include accession as well.

Nations that have not ratified the NPT are India, Pakistan, Israel, and North Korea. Nations that have not ratified the CWC are Egypt, Israel, and North Korea. And nations that have not ratified the BWC include Syria, Israel, and North Korea.

The ideal setup for a peaceful world envisages democratic nations that have ratified all the WMD treaties. Even a better world is conceivable. Given the historically-evidenced inclinations of the human species toward destruction, a better world without the WMD remains an elusive but a worthwhile ambition.

"Nations That Threatened the World," by L. Ali Khan, May 1, 2017.

- Being indoors during an airborne attack can lessen the exposure depending on the building. The degree of exposure for people inside a closed building when a biological or chemical plume passes outside is reduced by a factor of two or more for typical American homes and by a factor of as much as 10 or more for hermetically sealed office buildings, depending on the quality of the air filters in the heating, ventilation, and air conditioning system.

Producers of Biological Weapons

Offensive biological weapons programs reportedly exist today in a dozen countries, particularly in the Middle East and Asia. Countries currently listed as "proliferation concerns" by the Henry L. Stimson Center, a think tank in Washington, DC, include China, Egypt, Iran, Iraq, Israel, Libya, North Korea, Syria, and Taiwan.

- China continues to maintain some elements of an offensive biological weapons program that it is believed to have started in the 1950s. It possesses biotechnology infrastructure sufficiently advanced to allow it to develop and produce biological agents. Its munitions industry is sufficient to allow it to weaponize such agents, and it has a variety of means that could be used for delivery.

- China's offensive biological warfare capability is believed to be based on technology developed before its accession in 1984 to the Biological and Toxin Weapons Convention (BWC). Since then, China has claimed that it has never researched, produced, or possessed any biological weapons and would never do so. Nevertheless, its declarations under the BWC guidelines for confidence-building purposes are believed to be inaccurate and incomplete.

- India has many well-qualified scientists, numerous biological and pharmaceutical production facilities, and biocontainment facilities suitable for research and development of dangerous pathogens. At least some of these facilities are being used to support research and development for biological warfare defense work.

- Iran has a growing biotechnology industry, significant pharmaceutical experience, and the overall infrastructure to support a biological warfare program. Tehran has expanded its efforts to seek considerable dual-use biotechnical materials and expertise from entities in Russia and elsewhere, ostensibly for civilian purposes. Outside assistance, which Iran needs, is difficult to prevent because of the dual-use nature of the materials and equipment it seeks and the many legitimate end uses for these items.

- Iran's biological weapons program began during the Iran-Iraq war. Iran is believed to be pursuing offensive biological warfare capabilities, and its effort may have evolved beyond agent research and development to the ability to produce small quantities of agents.

- Libya ratified the BWC but has continued its biological warfare program. The program has not advanced significantly beyond research and development, though it may be capable of producing small quantities of biological agents. It has been hindered by a poor scientific and technological base, equipment shortages, a lack of skilled personnel, and UN sanctions from 1992 to 1999.

- Without foreign assistance and technical expertise on dual-use materials, Libya's biological warfare program is not likely to make significant progress. However, with the suspension of UN sanctions, Libya's ability to acquire biological-related equipment and expertise will increase.

- North Korea has acceded to the BWC but nonetheless has pursued biological warfare capabilities since the 1960s. Pyongyang's resources include a rudimentary (by Western standards) biotechnical infrastructure that could support the production of infectious biological warfare agents and toxins such as anthrax, cholera, and plague. North Korea is believed to possess a munitions-production infrastructure that would allow it to weaponize biological warfare agents, and it may have biological weapons available for use.

- Pakistan is believed to have the resources and capabilities to support limited biological warfare research and development. It may continue to seek foreign equipment and technology to expand its biotechnical infrastructure. Pakistan has ratified the BWC and participates actively in compliance protocol negotiations.

- Iraq is known to have manufactured relatively large quantities of anthrax and botulinum toxins; however, its scientists apparently have had difficulty developing efficient spray nozzles, forcing them to rely on explosive release by Scud missiles equipped with these toxins. Iraq may have produced up to 10 billion doses of anthrax, botulinum toxin, and aflatoxin.

- Under supervision by the UN team of inspectors (UNSCOM), 38,537 filled and unfilled munitions, 690 tons of agents, 3,000 tons of chemical precursors to chemical weapons agents, and thousands of pieces of production equipment and analytical instruments were destroyed in Iraq before UNSCOM was expelled in December 1998. Since then, no complete accounting of Iraq's chemical weapons program has been possible.

- Moreover:

  1. Iraq had removed chemical weapons, equipment, and materials from the main site of the al-Muthanna State Establishment before the first UNSCOM inspection team arrived in June 1991; no full accounting of these materials has been forthcoming.

  2. Iraq's claims that it has destroyed 15,620 chemical munitions are unverified. It also has provided no documentation regarding 16,038 chemical munitions it claims to have discarded.

3. UNSCOM inspectors reportedly were closing in on an Iraqi program for the production of VX, a deadly chemical agent, when the standoff between Iraq and the UN Security Council began in the autumn of 1997. In November 1997, the inspectors found new evidence that Iraq had obtained at least 750 tons of VX precursor chemicals. Evidence of VX production was first revealed in 1995.

Comparative Effects of Different Bioterrorist Attacks

Various government and defense-related studies on the potential effects of nuclear, chemical, or biological attacks on the United States have been conducted. Much of this information is available to the intelligence and policy communities, as well as the American public and those who would harm them.

In 1993, for example, an expert at the Office of Technology Assessment (OTA), a now-defunct arm of the US Congress, released his assessment of the damage that could be caused in two scenarios based on the method of delivery.

Scenario #1: Agents Delivered by Missile Warheads
This scenario assumes that an agent successfully reaches US soil aboard one Scud-sized warhead with a maximum payload of 1,000 kilograms. The study also assumes that the maximum use of this payload capability was not used. It is unclear whether this assumption is realistic.

Scenario #2: Agents Delivered by One Aircraft
This scenario assumes that the agents are delivered by one aircraft carrying 1,000 kilograms (kg) of Sarin nerve gas or 100 kg of anthrax spores. It assumes the aircraft flies in a straight line over the target at optimal altitude and dispenses the agent as an aerosol. It also assumes that maximum use of this payload capability was not used. It is unclear whether this last assumption is realistic.

Economic and Other Effects

Even the mere threat of a bioagricultural attack could have a devastating effect on the economy. For example, an anonymous caller to the US embassy in Santiago, Chile, in 1989 claimed that Chilean grapes destined for US and Japanese markets were contaminated with cyanide. The United States placed a quarantine on Chilean grapes and forced the growers to recall those that had been shipped, causing approximately $333 million in damage to the Chilean grape industry.

Government Estimates of the Impact. Several official reports highlight the risk posed to Americans and the effects such attacks would have on the US economy.

- The CDC has estimated that an anthrax attack by a terrorist would result in an economic impact of $477.8 million to $26.2 billion for every 100,000 persons exposed.

- A 1993 OTA report estimated that 250 pounds of anthrax spores, spread efficiently over the Washington, DC, metropolitan area, could cause up to 3 million deaths, more than from a 1-megaton hydrogen bomb.

- A senior-level war game in June 2001, called "Dark Winter," looked at the national security, intergovernmental, and information challenges of a biological attack on the US homeland. One conclusion of the war game, hosted by the Center for Strategic and International Studies, the Johns Hopkins Center for Civilian Biodefense Studies, the ANSER Institute for Homeland Security, and the Oklahoma National Memorial Institute for the Prevention of Terrorism: Within three months of a biological attack on Oklahoma City using smallpox, over 3 million Americans could be infected, and over a million would be killed.

- Moreover, the study concluded:

   [A]n attack on the United States with biological weapons could threaten vital national security interests. Massive civilian casualties, breakdown in essential institutions, violation of democratic processes, civil disorder, loss of confidence in government and reduced US strategic flexibility abroad are among the ways a biological attack might compromise US security.

- According to a US Army study, a Scud missile (launched at a US city from a ship lying outside US territorial waters carrying a warhead filled with botulinum could contaminate an area of 3,700 square km if weather conditions were ideal and an effective dispersal mechanism was available. This is 16 times greater than the reach of the same warhead filled with Sarin gas. By the time symptoms began to appear, treatment would have little chance of success; rapid field detection methods for biological warfare agents do not yet exist.

Is the Government Prepared?

The President's decision to create an Office of Homeland Security, headed by former Pennsylvania Governor Tom Ridge, is timely. The office is tasked with coordinating government efforts to stop all forms of terrorism, including biological attacks, before they occur and responding to an attack once it does occur.

According to a recent US General Accounting Office (GAO) report, coordination of federal terrorism research, preparedness, and the responsible programs thus far has been fragmented. Several agencies are responsible for coordinating functions, and this both limits accountability and hinders unity of effort. Moreover, several agencies have not been included in bioterrorism-related policy and response planning meetings, and different agencies have developed lists of biological agents as well as disaster response assistance programs for state and local governments. The Federal Emergency Management Agency (FEMA), the Department of Justice, the CDC, and the Office of Emergency Preparedness (OEP), for example, offer separate assistance to state and local governments in planning for emergencies that include bioterrorism.

Evidence that efforts at the federal, state, and local levels need to be coordinated can be found in various reports and government activities.

- The Advisory Committee on Immunization Practices has recommended anthrax vaccinations for military personnel who are deployed to high-risk areas.

- An interagency health care group, led by the US Department of Health and Human Services (HHS), chose four biological agents for the CDC to begin developing vaccine stockpiles for civilian populations. These are inhalation anthrax, pneumonic plague, smallpox, and tularemia, which have the ability to affect large numbers of people and to tax the medical system should bioterrorism occur.

- The CDC's bioterrorism program, which formally began in 1999, did not receive funding until fiscal year 2001 ($9.2 million). The CDC established the National Pharmaceutical Stockpile in FY 1999 to maintain "push packages"—prepackaged containers comprised of pharmaceuticals, intravenous and airway supplies, emergency medications, bandages and dressings. These are to be delivered to any US location to counter the effects of nerve agents, biological pathogens, and chemical agents within 12 hours of a decision to send them. The packages were deployed for the first time following the September 11 attacks in New York.

- The Clinton Administration's FY 2000 budget request included over $10 billion in non-Department of Defense efforts to combat terrorism. It requested almost $1.4 billion for law enforcement programs to address terrorist threats from chemical, biological, radiological, or nuclear weapons. This amount exceeded what the Clinton Administration requested (less than $1 billion) for military programs to counter chemical and biological threats.

- Spending on HHS's bioterrorism initiative has increased from $7 million in FY 1996 to $348 million for FY 2002, an 18 percent increase over last year's request. This includes $76.7 million for the CDC to upgrade state and local capacities to identify bioterrorist agents, including the development of diagnostic methods and technology investment.

- The OEP, the Department of Veterans Affairs (VA), and the Marine Corps Chemical and Biological Incident Response Force (CBIRF) have not had basic internal controls to help them manage their stockpiles of antidotes and antibiotics. A recent inventory identified a number of items that were stocked below their required levels or that had expired, as well as excesses of other items like sterile gloves. In one location, 1,000 fewer diazepam injectors than the amount required in an emergency were found.

- In May 2001, President Bush ordered Vice President Richard Cheney to conduct an interagency effort to correct deficiencies in coordinating a response to an attack with weapons of mass destruction.

- A GAO study released in September 2001 concluded that the Attorney General's Five-Year Interagency Counterterrorism and Technology Crime Plan, issued in December 1998, could serve as the basis for a national strategy. According to the GAO, however, it lacks two critical elements: measurable outcomes and identification of state and local government roles in responding to a terrorist incident.

As these reports show, government agencies have begun to look more closely at the threat of biological terrorism, and some have already instituted policies and programs to prevent such attacks or limit the damage should one occur. However, numerous loopholes still exist. The Achilles' heel of government programs to combat bioterrorism will be a lack of real coordination through a national strategy that outlines the roles of federal, state, and local agencies after an attack. Without such a strategy, the risk for chaos increases as does the likelihood that resources will be squandered by overlapping efforts and insufficient bureaucratic attention.

Governor Ridge's greatest challenge as Assistant to the President for Homeland Security will be to untangle the web of agencies and programs responsible for responding to a biological attack so that he can efficiently coordinate a national response to biological terrorism in the future.

Conclusion

Terrorist organizations prey on deficiencies in national infrastructure and planning. The United States lacks a coordinated and tested mechanism for responding to a biological or chemical attack, and this deficiency invites terrorists to develop the means to use these deadly weapons.

President Bush recently took a significant step toward eliminating this problem by creating the Office [of] Homeland Security. But as these facts and figures show, even though bioterrorists will face difficulties in carrying out a biological attack against America, it is well within their grasp to do so. And as the terrible events of September 11 demonstrate, the United States is far from invulnerable to those who wish it harm.

The Administration and Congress are wise to conduct a war on terrorism while pursuing a homeland defense strategy that will reduce the risk of bioterrorism and limit devastation should an attack occur.

Throughout the World Many Countries Possess or Have Possessed Chemical and Biological Weapons

Daryl Kimball

In the following viewpoint, Daryl Kimball maintains that many countries around the world either have possessed, are researching or developing, or have used chemical and biological weapons. The author outlines the past and present conditions of chemical and biological weapons in this staggering list of countries, including the United States, which continues to research such weapons. Kimball is the executive director of the Arms Control Association and is an expert on biological and chemical weapons.

As you read, consider the following questions:

1. Which type of weapon has seen a better sign-on for prevention of use according to the viewpoint?
2. How many "states" have not signed on or ratified the BWC as reported by Kimball?
3. As of 2016, has the US destroyed all of its chemical weapons?

"Chemical and Biological Weapons Status at a Glance," by Daryl Kimball, Arms Control Association, June 2018. https://www.armscontrol.org/factsheets/cbwprolif. Reprinted by permission.

D espite the progress made by international conventions, biological weapons (BW) and chemical weapons (CW) still pose a threat.

More progress has been made by Chemical Weapons Convention (CWC) states-parties and the Organization for the Prohibition of Chemical Weapons (OPCW) in the destruction of declared CW stockpiles. Progress on the implementation of the Biological Weapons Convention (BWC), however, has been slower due to the lack of a formal verification mechanism.

There are 180 states parties to the BWC, including Palestine, and six signatories (Central African Republic, Egypt, Haiti, Somalia, Syria, and Tanzania). Eleven states have neither signed nor ratified the BWC (Chad, Comoros, Djibouti, Eritrea, Israel, Kiribati, Micronesia, Niue, Namibia, Niue, South Sudan and Tuvalu).

There are 193 states parties to the Chemical Weapons Convention. Israel has signed but not ratified the convention and Egypt, North Korea, South Sudan have neither signed nor ratified the CWC.

Below is a list of states believed to currently possess or have once possessed biological and/or chemical weapons and their current status. Some states have officially declared BW or CW programs, while other programs have been alleged to exist by other states. Therefore, both official declarations and unofficial allegations of chemical and biological weapons programs are included below.

Albania

Chemical Weapons

State declaration: Although it joined the CWC in 1994, Albania did not acknowledge its possession of 16 metric tons of mustard agent (as well as small quantities of lewisite and other chemicals) until 2003. The OPCW declared Albania's destruction complete in July 2007.

China

Biological Weapons

State declaration: China states that it is in compliance with its BWC obligations and that it has never had an active BW program.

Allegations: According to the United States, China's BW activities have been extensive and a 1993 State Department Compliance Report alleged that activities continued after China joined the BWC. The 2010 report indicates that little information is known about China's activities, and that recent dual-use activities may have breached the BWC. Existing infrastructure would allow it to develop, produce, and weaponize agents. The 2017 report does not discuss China's BWC compliance or noncompliance.

Chemical Weapons

State declaration: China states that it is in compliance with the CWC. China declared in 1997 that it had a small offensive CW program that has now been dismantled, which has been verified by over 400 inspections by the OPCW as of 2016.

Allegations: The US alleged in 2003, that China has an "advanced chemical weapons research and development program." However, these allegations have decreased in magnitude in recent years and the State Department's 2017 report on compliance with the CWC cited no such concerns.

Other information: Approximately 350,000 chemical munitions were left on Chinese soil by Japan during the Second World War. Work with Japan to dispose of these is ongoing.

Cuba

Biological Weapons

State declaration: Cuba denies any BW research efforts.

Allegations: A 2003 State Department Compliance Report indicated that Cuba had "at least a limited developmental offensive biological warfare research and development effort." The 2010 report claimed that "available information did not indicate Cuba's dual-use activities during the reporting period involved activities prohibited by the BWC." The 2017 report did not mention any problems with Cuba's compliance with BWC.

Allegations of BW programs have been made by Cuban defectors in the past.

Other information: Cuba has relatively advanced biotechnology industrial capabilities.

Egypt

Biological Weapons

State declaration: Two vague statements alluding to a BW capability were made by President Sadat and one of his ministers in 1972, but Egypt has not officially declared a biological weapons stockpile.

Allegations: There have been various allegations that Egypt possesses biological weapons. Some argue that Egypt's reluctance to ratify the BWC signals that it does possess biological weapons. The 2014 State Department compliance report notes that Egypt has "continued to improve its biotechnology infrastructure" over the past three years, including through research and development activities involving genetic engineering, as of 2013's end, "available information did not indicate that Egypt is engaged in activities prohibited by the BWC." The 2017 State Department report does not mention any problems with Egypt's compliance with the BWC.

Chemical Weapons

Allegations: There is strong evidence that Egypt employed bombs and artillery shells filled with phosgene and mustard agents during the Yemen Civil War from (1963–1967) but it is unclear if Egypt currently possesses chemical weapons. In 1989, the United States and Switzerland alleged that Egypt was producing chemical weapons in a plant north of Cairo. As a non-party to the CWC, Egypt has not had to issue any formal declarations about CW programs and capabilities.

India

Chemical Weapons

State declaration: India declared in June 1997 that it possessed a CW stockpile of 1,044 metric tons of mustard agent. India completed destruction of its stockpile in 2009.

Iran

Biological Weapons

State declaration: Iran has publicly denounced BW.

Allegations: The Defense Intelligence Agency alleged in 2009 that Iran's BW efforts "may have evolved beyond agent R&D, and we believe Iran likely has the capability to produce small quantities of BW agents but may only have a limited ability to weaponize them."

The 2010 report assesses that there is evidence showing Iran continues dual-use activities, but there is no conclusive evidence showing BWC violations. The 2017 State Department report on compliance with the BWC does not mention any problems with Iran's compliance with the BWC.

Chemical Weapons

State declaration: Iran has denounced the possession and use of CW in international forums.

Allegations: Pre-2003 US intelligence assessments alleged that Iran had a stockpile of CW. This stockpile is thought to have included blister, blood, and choking agents and probably nerve agents. After 2003, however, the United States stopped making such allegations. The United States claimed it was unable to ascertain if Iran is meeting its obligations under the CWC, according to a State Department 2017 report on compliance with the CWC.

Other information: Iran suffered tens of thousands of casualties from Iraqi use of chemical weapons during the1980–1988 Iran-Iraq War. Iran's CW program is believed to have been started after Iraqi CW use. There are no known credible allegations that Iran used any chemical weapons against Iraq in response.

Iraq

Biological Weapons

State declaration: Iraq admitted to testing and stockpiling BW in the mid-1990s. These stockpiles appear to have been destroyed prior to the 2003 invasion. There have been no declarations about BW after 2003.

Chemical Weapons

State declaration: Iraq had an extensive chemical weapons program before the Persian Gulf War dating back to the 1960s under which it produced and stockpiled mustard, tabun, sarin, and VX. Iraq delivered chemical agents against Iranian forces during the Iran-Iraq War using aerial bombs, artillery, rocket launchers, tactical rockets, and helicopter-mounted sprayers and it also used chemical weapons against its Kurdish population in 1988. Its program was largely dismantled by United Nations weapons inspectors in the 1990s.

Iraq declared in August 1998 that it had dismantled all of its chemical weapons in partnership with the UN Special Commission established for that purpose.

Iraq then submitted an additional declaration to the OPCW of an unknown quantity of chemical weapons remnants contained in two storage bunkers in March 2009. Destruction activities were delayed due to an unstable security situation, but began in 2017. On March 13, 2018, the OPCW announced that all of Iraq's chemical weapons had been destroyed.

Israel

Biological Weapons

State declaration: Israel has revealed little in terms of its biological weapons capabilities or programs.

Allegations: There is belief that Israel has had an offensive BW program in the past. It is unclear if this is still the case.

Chemical Weapons

Allegations: Some allege that Israel had an offensive CW program in the past. It is unclear if Israel maintains an ongoing program.

Libya

Biological Weapons

State declaration: Libya announced in December 2003 that it would eliminate its BW program.

Allegations: Between 1982 and 2003, there were many allegations of a Libyan biological weapons program, although later inspections failed to reveal any evidence to support these claims.

Chemical Weapons

State declaration: In 2003, Libya announced it would be abandoning its CW program, and in 2004, it declared possession of chemical agents and facilities. Libya declared 24.7 metric tons of mustard agent in bulk containers. In addition, it declared one inactivated chemical weapons production facility, two chemical weapons storage sites, 1,300 metric tons of precursor chemicals, and 3,563 unfilled aerial bombs. Libya completed the destruction of its Category 1 chemical weapons in January 2014. With assistance from the OPCW and other member states, Libya removed all of the remaining chemical weapons from its territory for destruction in August 2016. In January 2018, the OPCW declared that Libya's entire chemical weapons arsenal had been destroyed.

North Korea

Biological Weapons

Allegations: The 2010 State Department report on compliance with the BWC remarks that North Korea may "still consider the use of biological weapons as a military option." In a 2012 Ministry of National Defense White Paper, South Korea asserted that "North Korea likely has the capability to produce … anthrax, smallpox, pest, francisella tularensis, and hemorrhagic fever viruses."

Chemical Weapons

Allegations: North Korea is widely believed to possess a large chemical stockpile including nerve, blister, choking, and blood agents. The 2012 unclassified intelligence assessment provided to Congress states that North Korea has a "long standing CW program" and "possesses a large stockpile of agents." In February 2017, North Korean agents used VX, a nerve agent, to assassinate Kim Jong Nam, the half-brother of Kim Jong Un, in Malaysia.

Russia

Biological Weapons

State declaration: In January 1992, Boris Yeltsin acknowledged that the Soviet Union had pursued an extensive and offensive BW program throughout the 1970s and 1980s. However, since joining the BWC in 1992, Russia has repeatedly expressed its commitment to the destruction of its biological weapons.

Allegations: The Soviet Union's extensive offensive germ program included weaponized tularemia, typhus, Q fever, smallpox, plague, anthrax, Venezuelan equine encephalitis, glanders, brucellosis, and Marburg. The Soviet Union also researched numerous other agents and toxins that can attack humans, plants, and livestock.

The United States has repeatedly expressed concern about Russia's inherited biological weapons program and uncertainty about Russia's compliance with the BWC.

The 2010 State Department report on compliance with the BWC details that Russia continues to engage in dual-use biological research activities, yet there is no evidence that such work is inconsistent with BWC obligations. It assesses that it remains unclear whether Russia has fulfilled its obligations under Article I of the convention. The 2017 report states that "Russia's annual BWC CBM submissions since 1992 have not satisfactorily documented whether the BW items under these programs were destroyed or diverted to peaceful purposes, as required by Article II of the BWC."

Chemical Weapons

State declaration: Russia possessed the world's largest chemical weapons stockpile: approximately 40,000 metric tons of chemical agent, including VX, sarin, soman, mustard, lewisite, mustard-lewisite mixtures, and phosgene.

Russia has declared its arsenal to the OPCW and commenced destruction. Along with the United States, Russia received an extension when it was unable to complete destruction by the 2012 deadline imposed by the CWC. A 2016 OPCW report indicated that as of 2015, Russia had destroyed about 92 percent of its stockpile (around 36,7500 metric tons). On September 27, 2017, the OPCW announced that Russia completed destruction of its chemical weapons arsenal.

Allegations: The US has some reservations about Russian compliance with the CWC, as expressed in the 2017 State Department report on CWC compliance which stated, "The United States cannot certify that Russia has met its obligations under the Convention," and asserted that Russia had not made a complete declaration of its stockpile.

The UK accused Russia of assassinating a former Russian spy, Sergei Skripal, and his daughter Yulia, in the UK using the chemical agent Novichok on March 4, 2018.

South Korea

Chemical Weapons

State declaration: South Korea declared a chemical weapons stockpile of unspecified agents when it joined the CWC in 1997 and completed destruction of its declared arsenal on July 10, 2008. It does not admit publically that it possessed chemical weapons and was noted in OPCW materials as a "state party."

Sudan

Chemical Weapons

State declaration: After acceding to the CWC in 1999, Sudan declared only a small selection of unspecified riot control agents.

Allegations: There are unconfirmed reports that Sudan developed and used CW in the past. The US bombed an alleged CW factory in 1998. There have been no serious allegations in recent years. Sudan was not included in the 2017 State Department report on compliance with the CWC.

Syria

Biological Weapons

State declaration: In July 2012, a spokesman for the Syrian Foreign Ministry confirmed that the country possesses biological warfare materials, but little is known about the extent of the arsenal. On July 14, 2014, Syria declared the existence of production facilities and stockpiles of purified ricin, although little is known about the continued existence of such facilities in 2017.

Chemical Weapons

State declaration: On September 20, 2013, Syria submitted a declaration of its chemical weapons and facilities to the OPCW after years of denying the program's existence. The OPCW announced that the entirety of Syria's declared stockpile of 1,308 metric tons of sulfur mustard agent and precursor chemicals had been destroyed in January 2016. However, reports continue to surface of chemical weapon use in Syria, raising questions about the accuracy of its initial declaration.

Allegations: Syria had an extensive program producing a variety of agents, including nerve agents such as sarin and VX, and blistering agents, according to governments and media sources. There were also some allegations of deployed CW on SCUD missiles. Several UN-OPCW Joint Investigative Mechanism (JIM) reports have found that the Syrian government was responsible for chemical weapons attacks in Syria, including in April 2014, March 2015, March 2016, and April 2017 and that the Islamic State was responsible for chemical weapons attacks in Syria in August 2015 and September 2016.

Taiwan
Chemical Weapons
State declaration: Taiwan has declared that it possesses small quantities of CW for research but denies any weapons possession.

The United States
Biological Weapons
State declaration: The United States unilaterally gave up its biological weapons program in 1969. The destruction of all offensive BW agents occurred between 1971 and 1973. The United States currently conducts research as part of its biodefense program.

Allegations: According to a compliance report published by the Russian government in August 2010, the United States is undertaking research on Smallpox which is prohibited by the World Health Organization. Russia also accused the United States of undertaking BW research in order to improve defenses against bio-terror attacks which is "especially questionable from the standpoint of Article I of the BTWC."

Chemical Weapons
State declaration: The United States declared a large chemical arsenal of 27,770 metric tons to the OPCW after the CWC came into force in 1997. Along with Russia, the United States received an extension when it was unable to complete destruction of its chemical stockpiles by 2012. A 2016 OPCW report declared that the United States had destroyed approximately 90 percent of the chemical weapons stockpile it had declared as the CWC entered into force; nearly 25,000 metric tons of the declared total

of 27,770. The United States has destroyed all of Category 2 and Category 3 weapons and is projected to complete destruction of its Category 1 weapons by 2023.

Allegations: A 2010 Russian report alleged that the United States has legislation which could inhibit inspections and investigations of US chemical facilities. Russia has also accused the United States of not fully reporting chemical agents removed from Iraq between 2003 and 2008 and sent to the United States for testing and subsequent destruction.

Could Biological Agents Gain Traction as Weapons?

Oliver Meier

In the following viewpoint, Oliver Meier argues that in general, the use of biological weapons appears to have waned, and in fact such weapons have not been used during conflicts since World War II. But the author also contends that, for various reasons, biological agents could again become players in the global weapon arena. Meier writes for the German Institute for International and Security Affairs.

As you read, consider the following questions:

1. According to the author what does the BWC prohibit?
2. As stated by the viewpoint, which two countries may be using or developing biological weapons?
3. What gene technology may make biological weapons attractive to use?

The world is a safer place thanks to the effective implementation of the Biological and Toxin Weapons Convention (BWC). The convention, which was opened for signature in 1972, prohibits the development, production, acquisition, and storage of biological weapons. While chemical weapons are being used in Syria and it is uncertain whether the Iran nuclear agreement will continue to block Tehran's path to the nuclear bomb, all seems quiet on the biological weapons front.

No biological weapons have been used in conflict since World War II. United Nations Special Commission inspectors dismantled Iraq's biological weapons program in the early 1990s. The huge Soviet biological weapons program was officially shut down in 1990. There have been zero fatalities from biological weapons since the 2001 anthrax attacks in the United States Anthrax attacks in the United States. Furthermore, no country admits to having a biological weapons program. Most importantly, there is a strong feeling that the deliberate use of disease for hostile purposes is abhorrent. The taboo against biological warfare remains intact.

Challenges

Given the nonuse of biological weapons over the years and widespread state disinterest in pursuing them, it should follow that the eighth BWC review conference, to be held November 7–25, should be an unremarkable affair. However, three structural problems threaten to undermine existing international norms against the use of bioweapons and biological warfare.

First, the assumption that biological weapons, when compared to chemical or nuclear weapons, are militarily unattractive should be reassessed. A surprising finding of the international investigation into Syria's chemical weapons program was that Damascus, which is a signatory to the BWC but has not ratified it, had a production facility for ricin, a toxin whose misuse is prohibited under the BWC and Chemical Weapons Convention. This was the first time in twenty years that a state had been found to be working on biological weapons. While Syria claims that its ricin program had served peaceful purposes and its failure to declare the program was an oversight, there is insufficient information to know the real rationale for the program. However, Syria's unconventional uses of chemical weapons, as a tool of terror, coercion, and influence in its civil war, should lead the BWC states parties to consider the possibility that states might be open to using biological weapons beyond deterrence and intrastate warfare. Keep in mind that North Korea may also be working on biological weapons.

Second, biotechnology is making tremendous leaps forward, and emerging technologies, such as CRISPR [gene editing], could increase the military attractiveness of biological weapons. Future biowarfare may be less about infecting people with deadly or debilitating diseases than manipulating the way humans function. Thus, future misuse of biotechnology may differ from what the original BWC drafters imagined as the primary role of bioweapons. For example, state-sponsored bioterrorism similar to South Africa's biological weapons program in the 1980s, which was aimed at the development of toxins to kill the regime's political opponents, could be among the threats that at this moment do not appear prominently on decision-makers' radars.

Third, the threat of nonstate actors using biological weapons is growing. Until recently, the risk of a bioterrorism attack by nonstate actors appeared to be greatly exaggerated. However, well-funded and [well]-organized groups like the self-proclaimed Islamic State may now hold sufficient territory for long enough to enable them to develop and use biological weapons.

Forum or Treaty? Different Visions for the BWC

Seen by themselves, none of these challenges are new, but their convergence multiplies the risk that biological weapons might be considered weapons of war. Yet the responses of BWC states parties to these trends are similar to what they had been in the past. Since the collapse in 2001 of talks on a BWC verification and compliance protocol, two evolving visions for the BWC have framed discussions at meetings of states parties.

Broadly speaking, the United States and other Western states see the convention primarily as a forum where states can discuss and elaborate joint measures to address the deliberate or accidental spread of disease. For Washington, the BWC is part of its broader global health security agenda. According to this view, the convention should be a place to set standards for national measures; discuss best practices on issues such as biosecurity; and facilitate assistance for states that have insufficient capacities to establish stricter domestic checks on dangerous pathogens. To be sure, these are important measures, but they are insufficient to address the dangers of military misuse of biotechnology by governments or international terrorist networks.

Others still see the BWC through the lens of a classical arms control instrument. Russia, for example, has recently revived ideas to negotiate a legally binding protocol to the BWC. Nonaligned states emphasize the need to close the verification gap, which sets the BWC apart from the Chemical Weapons Convention and Nuclear Nonproliferation Treaty. Those behind the push to resume talks on a BWC verification protocol may not be pursuing the idea seriously. They know that Western states hold divergent ideas on how to move forward. For example, the EU still maintains that verification "remains a central element of a complete and effective disarmament and nonproliferation regime," while the United States has rejected the notion that compliance with the BWC can be effectively monitored. By pushing such proposals, Russia and nonaligned states may hope to expose such differences. But even if there are no ulterior motives behind these ideas, such a course of action is not well suited to take into account the transnational and technological dynamics that threaten the foundations of the BWC.

What to Expect

It is far from clear that states parties' representatives at the November [2016] review conference will be able or willing to bridge these fundamental differences on the future of the BWC. The antagonism between Russia and the West, the uncompromising position of some key nonaligned states, and the lack of willingness of moderate groupings, such as the European Union, to play a lead role in refreshing and bolstering the convention make it unlikely that there will be a coordinated push for a major overhaul of the BWC.

The timing of the conference is also a complicating factor. The opening of the review conference coincides with the US presidential elections. News about the next US administration will not only be a distraction, but could also make it harder for the US delegation to commit to any new, substantive measures.

Given this complicated picture, it is difficult to conceive of a scenario in which BWC states parties would be willing to agree to a thorough review of the threats and urgently needed measures to update the regime's instruments. States parties at the review conference should therefore aim first at refocusing the convention on its core purpose, prohibiting the hostile use of biotechnology. Secondly, representatives should strengthen the treaty's decision-making procedures so that the regime becomes more operational and less deliberative. Four measures would be useful toward these ends.

First, the most important task of the review conference is to reconfirm the comprehensive prohibition of all types of misuse of biological agents and toxins based on the "general-purpose criterion," which defines the scope of the convention. States parties must make it clear that gray zones do not exist. They should clearly state that tinkering with genes and developing novel means of biological-agent delivery and other burgeoning biological technologies are all prohibited unless they serve prophylactic, protective, or other peaceful purposes. Moreover, additional transparency measures would be useful to reduce the risk of misperception about the intentions behind biodefense programs. Second, states parties should exercise caution when tinkering with the scope of the BWC. Russia has recently proposed creating a new convention to suppress acts of biological and chemical terrorism. It is unclear whether this proposed convention would compete with or complement the BWC. Likewise, the US approach of discussing the BWC as one of many instruments to tackle threats at the intersection of security and global health may also be problematic. It could lead to a loss of focus, particularly because other scientific communities have begun to see the BWC as a useful platform to advance their own agendas.

Third, numerous state parties have expressed support for a regular, independent review of scientific and technological developments. The review conference could launch a scientific advisory committee comprised of experts that report annually on scientific developments relevant to the BWC.

Fourth, institutional reform of the treaty's bodies is urgently needed. Currently, binding decisions can only be made at the review conference, which is only held every five years. This snail's pace of diplomacy is an anachronism. It suits only those that are opposed to flexible and strong international control mechanisms. Among other things, the review conference should empower annual meetings of states parties to address compliance concerns and to make decisions, including on additional transparency measures and the applicability of the treaty's prohibitions to new technologies. Such an annual review would make the BWC more adaptable and could trigger higher-level diplomacy. To support this process, states parties should upgrade the Implementation Support Unit, which is a meagerly staffed, three-person secretariat already strained by providing necessary support for BWC implementation by states parties.

Unfortunately, the above measures would still be insufficient to address the need of a BWC compliance mechanism. Monitoring treaty compliance is hampered by the lack of a dedicated permanent organization to implement the convention. This major deficiency sets the BWC apart from treaties like the Chemical Weapons Convention, which has the Organisation for the Prohibition of Chemical Weapons. In the long term, a mix of tried and tested instruments and methods as well as new ones will have to be created to verify BWC compliance, follow up on violations of the treaty, implement the convention, and foster the further evolution of the regime. At the very least, states parties at the eighth review conference in November should begin to work toward this goal.

In the United States Counterterrorism Experts Expect WMD Attacks by Al-Qaeda

Rolf Mowatt-Larssen

In the following viewpoint, Rolf Mowatt-Larssen contends that al-Qaeda is on a mission to acquire weapons capable of doing great harm to a large portion of the US population. He argues that this terrorist group is concentrating their efforts on nuclear and biological weapons. Mowatt-Larssen maintains that al-Qaeda is concentrating its efforts to produce an attack that would be on a greater scale than that of 9/11. Mowatt-Larssen is an expert on weapons of mass destruction and director of the Intelligence Project at the Belfer Center at Harvard Kennedy School.

As you read, consider the following questions:

1. As defined in the viewpoint, what is a WMD?
2. What biological agent did al-Qaeda seek to develop for use after 9/11 according to the author?
3. According to the viewpoint, could bioterrorism be phony rhetoric?

Several terrorist groups have actively sought weapons of mass destruction (WMD) of one kind or another. In particular,

"Al Qaeda Weapons of Mass Destruction Threat: Hype or Reality?" by Rolf Mowatt-Larssen, Belfer Center for Science and International Affairs, January 2010. Reprinted by permission.

the Japanese cult group Aum Shinrikyo, al-Qaeda and its associates—notably the Egyptian Islamic Jihad, Jemaah Islamiya and Lashkar al Tayyib—figure most prominently among the groups that have manifested some degree of intent, experimentation, and programmatic efforts to acquire nuclear, biological and chemical weapons. To date, however, al-Qaeda is the only group known to be pursuing a long-term, persistent and systematic approach to developing weapons to be used in mass casualty attacks.

Osama bin Ladin's assertion in 1998 that it was his Islamic duty to acquire weapons of mass destruction, ensured that the fulfillment of this intent would become a top priority for his lieutenants in the ensuing years. In an effort to explain his thinking to his followers, and to help guide their efforts, the al-Qaeda leader has offered a number of statements that provide a need and rationale for using weapons of mass destruction as a means of achieving the group's concrete and ambitious goals. Most recently, he promised in a 2007 video release to "escalate the killing and fighting against you (Americans)"—on grounds of destroying an international conspiracy to control the world—adding, "The capitalist system seeks to turn the entire world into a fiefdom of the major corporations under the label of globalization in order to protect democracy."

These statements should not be interpreted as empty rhetoric and idle threats: Osama bin Ladin has signaled a specific purpose for using WMD in al-Qaeda's quest to destroy the global status quo, and to create conditions more conducive to the overthrow of apostate regimes throughout the Islamic world. His argument is essentially that even weapons of mass destruction—which are outlawed under Islam—are a justifiable means of countering US hegemony. Osama bin Ladin's morality-based argument on the nature of the struggle between militant Islamists and the US-led coalition of secular forces focuses the group's planning on the acquisition of strategic weapons that can be used in mass casualty attacks, rather than on the production of tactical, more readily available weapons such as "dirty bombs," chemical agents, crude toxins and poisons.

In this light, it is not surprising that the group's top WMD priority has been to acquire nuclear and strategic biological weapons. Considering the potential that such weapons hold in fulfilling al-Qaeda's aspirations, their WMD procurement efforts have been managed at the most senior levels, under rules of strict compartmentalization from lower levels of the organization, and with central control over possible targets and timing of prospective attacks. In this sense, their approach has been "Muhammed Atta-like"—similar to the modus operandi Khaled Sheikh Mohammed employed in making preparations for the 9/11 attacks—as opposed to resembling the signature characterizing most terrorist attacks to which the world has become accustomed.

Al-Qaeda's patient, decade-long effort to steal or construct an improvised nuclear device (IND) flows from their perception of the benefits of producing the image of a mushroom cloud rising over a US city, just as the 9/11 attacks have altered the course of history. This lofty aim helps explains why al-Qaeda has consistently sought a bomb capable of producing a nuclear yield, as opposed to settling for the more expedient and realistic course of devising a "dirty bomb," or a radiological dispersal device.

Another 9/11-scale operational plot managed by the al-Qaeda core leadership was the development of anthrax for use in a mass casualty attack in the United States. The sophisticated anthrax project was run personally by al-Qaeda deputy chief Ayman Zawahiri, in parallel to the group's efforts to acquire a nuclear capability; anthrax was probably meant to serve as another means to achieve the same effect as using a nuclear bomb, given doubts that a nuclear option could be successfully procured. Notably, al-Qaeda's efforts to acquire a nuclear and biological weapons capability were concentrated in the years preceding September 11, 2001. Based on the timing and nature of their WMD-related activity in the 1990s, al-Qaeda probably anticipated using these means of mass destruction against targets in the US homeland in the intensified campaign they knew would follow the 9/11 attack.

There is no indication that the fundamental objectives that lie behind their WMD intent have changed over time.

On the other hand, the pursuit of crude toxins and poisons appears to have been of little interest to the al-Qaeda leadership, even though the production of such weapons is easier and thus might seem more attractive for potential use in attacks. Although experimentation and training in crude chemical agents and pathogens was standard fare in al-Qaeda's camps in Afghanistan before 9/11, their use in attacks appears to have been left to the initiative of individual cells and planners outside the direct supervision of the al-Qaeda core leadership. Prominent examples of small-scale chemical- and biological-related activity include Midhat al-Mursi's (aka Abu Khabab) basic training for operatives in the al-Qaeda camps in Afghanistan before 9/11; the Abu Musab al Zarqawi network's plotting to use ricin and cyanide in multiple attacks planned in Europe in late-2002 [to] early-2003; and a Bahraini terrorist cell's plot to use a crude cyanide gas device called the "mobtaker" (an Arabic word roughly meaning "invention") in an attack on the New York City subway in the same time frame.

In each of these cases, the evidence suggests that the al-Qaeda senior leadership was not directly involved or apparently even aware of attack preparations until late stages of planning. Moreover, there is no evidence that the al-Qaeda leadership regarded the use of crude toxins and poisons as being suitable for conducting what would amount to pin prick attacks on the United States; on the contrary, Zawahiri canceled the planned attack on the New York City subway for "something better," suggesting that a relatively easy attack utilizing tactical weapons would not achieve the goals the al-Qaeda leadership had set for themselves.

So, why hasn't a terrorist WMD attack happened since 9/11?

There are many plausible explanations for why the world has not experienced an al-Qaeda attack using chemical, biological, radiological or nuclear weapons, but it would be foolish to discount the possibility that such an event will occur in the future. To date, al-Qaeda's WMD programs may have been disrupted. This is in fact one likely explanation, given a sustained and ferocious counterterrorist response to 9/11 that largely destroyed al-Qaeda as the organization that existed before the fateful attack on the US. If so, terrorists must continue to be disrupted and denied a safe haven to reestablish the ability to launch a major strike on the US homeland, or elsewhere in the world.

Or perhaps, al-Qaeda operational planners have failed to acquire the kind of weapons they seek, because they are unwilling to settle for anything other than a large scale attack in the US. It would surely be hard for al-Qaeda to lower the bar they set on 9/11: What would constitute a worthy follow-up to 9/11, on their terms? What would they achieve through another attack? There are few weapons that would meet their expectations in this regard. It is extremely difficult to acquire a functioning nuclear bomb, or to steal enough weapons-usable material to build a bomb. And as al-Qaeda probably learned in trying to weaponize anthrax, biological pathogens may seem simple enough to produce, but such weapons are not easy to bottle up and control. To complicate matters further, an attack on the scale of 9/11 is more difficult to accomplish in an environment of heightened security and vigilance in the US.

But if Osama bin Ladin and his lieutenants had been interested in employing crude chemical, biological and radiological materials in small scale attacks, there is little doubt they could have done so by now. However, events have shown that the al-Qaeda leadership does not choose weapons based on how easy they are to acquire and use, be they conventional or unconventional weapons. They choose them based on the best means of destroying the specific targets that they have in mind. Al-Qaeda's reasoning thus runs counter to analytic convention that equates the ease of acquisition of chemical, biological or radiological weapons with an increasing likelihood of terrorist use—i.e., a terrorist attack employing crude weapons is therefore more likely than an attack using a nuclear or large scale biological weapon. In fact, it is the opposite: If perpetrating a large-scale attack serves as al-Qaeda's motivation for possessing WMD, not deterrence value, then the greatest threat is

North Korea's Biological Weapons

North Korean development of biological weapons both poses a serious potential threat to the United States and its strategic partners, and illustrates the broader dangers of proliferation. Biological weapons pose dangers that are growing steadily with the proliferation of the civil, dual-use, and military technologies that can be used to develop and manufacture biological weapons—such as genetic engineering and drones.

In theory, North Korea has rejected the development of biological weapons and advocates a "nuclear, chemical, and biological weapons free zone" in the Korean Peninsula. North Korea acceded to the Biological Weapons Convention on March 13, 1987, and has consistently denied that it has biological weapons ever since. It has accused the United States of using biological weapons in the Korean War, and more recently of sending Anthrax to South Korea as part of such an effort, proving "that the United States is a group of gangsters threatening human existence." North Korea has also clearly developed nuclear weapons, however, and has long possessed large stocks of chemical weapons. Its restraint in any area of military activity seems dubious at best.

This means that the United States must plan for the possibility that North Korea has biological weapons and will continue to develop more sophisticated weapons over time. There also is a significant amount of reporting that it does have ongoing biological weapons programs, and even the mere possibility that North Korean—or any other set of threats—biological weapons exist already presents major problems for US military planning, and already gives North Korea deterrent and strategic leverage.

Such weapons present major problems for intelligence collection and analysis in both peacetime and war. This is true at both the strategic level—which is illustrated at the end of this testimony—and the operational level. For example, they present unique challenges in attributing and characterizing attacks—particularly if they are used on distant targets, mirror natural disease, and are used at a time when no major crisis and period of tension exists with North Korea.

"More Than A Nuclear Threat: North Korea's Chemical, Biological, and Conventional Weapons," by Anthony H. Cordesman, CSIS Publications, March 22, 2018.

posed by the most effective and simple means of mass destruction, whether these means consist of nuclear, biological, or other forms of asymmetric weapons.

An examination of the 9/11 attack sheds light on al-Qaeda's reasoning behind the selection of specific weapons, and how that may apply to the role WMD plays in their thinking. Al-Qaeda opted to pursue a highly complex and artfully choreographed plot to strike multiple targets requiring the simultaneous hijacking of several 747 jumbo passenger aircraft, because using airplanes as weapons offered the best means of attacking the targets they intended to destroy. If conventional wisdom on assessing WMD terrorism threats had been applied to considering the likelihood of the 9/11 plot, analysts may well have concluded it never would have happened; at the time, it was simply hard to believe any terrorist group could pull off such an elaborate plot utilizing novel, unpredictable weapons that were so difficult to acquire.

Yet, WMD terrorism skeptics abound, and for understandable reasons. There is widespread suspicion in America and abroad that WMD terrorism is another phony threat being hyped for political purposes, and to stoke fears among the public. It is difficult to debunk this allegation, given the US government's lack of credibility in the case of Iraqi WMD. That said, WMD terrorism is not Iraqi WMD. The case that the WMD terrorism threat is real bears no association with the Iraqi intelligence failure whatsoever, in terms of the reliability of the sources of intelligence, the quality of the information that has been collected, and the weight of the evidence that lies at the heart of our understanding of the threat. If anything, the biases in WMD terrorism analysis tilt towards treating the absence of information as an absence of threat; this could become a vulnerability in the defenses, considering the very real possibility that there may be a terrorist plot in motion that has not been found.

On the other side of the spectrum, even for the most ardent believers in the threat posed by WMD terrorism, it must be acknowledged that much of the rhetoric expressed by the top levels of the group might be just that: mere saber rattling in an increasingly desperate bid to remain relevant, to frighten their enemies, and to rally their followers with promises of powerful weapons that will reverse their losses on the battlefield. It is also possible that al-Qaeda may be engaging in a classic deception ruse, hoping to misdirect their foe with fears of mass destruction, in order to preserve the element of surprise for the fulfillment of their true intentions.

There may be kernels of truth in each of these reasons as to why the world has not yet witnessed a terrorist WMD attack, which is at least a mild surprise, considering all that has come to pass since 2001. However, for purposes of making a clear-headed assessment of the threat, it may be useful to separate al-Qaeda's WMD activity into two streams, one consisting of the strategic programs managed under the direct supervision and management of the al-Qaeda core leadership, and the other consisting of tactical chemical, biological and radiological weapons development that was decentralized and pursued autonomously in various locations around the world as part of the "global jihad." On this basis, a more precise determination can be made on the actual threat posted by al-Qaeda, and other groups in each of these cases.

Fortunately, there is a body of historical information that provides a useful starting point for such an inquiry. Hopefully, an examination of WMD-associated information that is pertinent, but no longer sensitive, can help bridge the gaps in perceptions between the diehard believers and skeptics as to the true nature of the problem and the threat it may pose, not just in an al-Qaeda context today, but in the future as WMD terrorism takes on new forms involving new actors.

In June 2003, the US government issued a warning that there was a high probability of an al-Qaeda WMD attack sometime in the next two years. This report represented a high water mark in concerns related to al-Qaeda's WMD planning going back to the founding of the group. Why didn't an attack happen in the next two years? Was the threat hyped for political purposes? Was the intelligence assessment wrong? Or, was the threat neutralized? Some perspective into why the report was issued can be gleaned by examining some of the evidence that was available to US and international policymakers by the summer of 2003 concerning roughly fifteen years of al-Qaeda's efforts to acquire weapons of mass destruction. Presenting this chronology will hopefully allow the reader to develop a better feel for the threat posed by al-Qaeda's interest in WMD at that time, and use it as a basis to help determine whether the WMD terrorism threat is real.

Periodical and Internet Sources Bibliography

The following articles have been selected to supplement the diverse views presented in this chapter.

Peter Apps, "Commentary: The Next Super Weapon Could Be Biological," Reuters, April 19, 2017. https://www.reuters.com/article/us-biological-weaons-commentary-idUSKBN17L1SZ.

Kate Charlet, "The New Killer Pathogens," *Foreign Affairs*, May/June 2018. https://www.foreignaffairs.com/articles/2018-04-16/new-killer-pathogens.

Praveen Duddu, "The World's Most Dangerous Bioweapons," *Army Technology*, April 12, 2015. https://www.army-technology.com/features/featurethe-worlds-most-dangerous-bioweapons-4546207/.

Gerald L. Epstein, "Biosecurity 2011: Not a Year to Change Minds," *Bulletin of the Atomic Scientists*, January 1, 2012. https://thebulletin.org/2012/01/biosecurity-2011-not-a-year-to-change-minds/.

Josh Gabbatiss, "North Korean Defector's Blood 'Contains Signs of Anthrax Infection' Amid Concerns Over Biological Weapons," *Independent*, December 27, 2017. https://www.independent.co.uk/news/world/asia/north-korea-defector-anthrax-infection-blood-signs-biological-weapons-evidence-nuclear-testing-a8130456.html.

Giles Milton, "Winston Churchill's Shocking Use of Chemical Weapons," *The Guardian*, September 1, 2013. https://www.theguardian.com/world/shortcuts/2013/sep/01/winston-churchill-shocking-use-chemical-weapons.

Norman Pearlstine, "Kim Jong Un," *Time*, 2017. http://time.com/time-person-of-the-year-2017-kim-jong-un-runner-up/.

Lizzy Tomei, "Why Chemical Weapons Are So Dangerous," *PRI*, December 6, 2012. https://www.pri.org/stories/2012-12-06/why-chemical-weapons-are-so-dangerous.

CHAPTER 2

The Effects of Chemical and Biological Warfare

In Russia Law Enforcement's Use of Chemical Agents on Innocent Civilians Is a Slippery Slope

Michael Crowley and Malcolm Dando

In the following viewpoint, Michael Crowley and Malcolm Dando argue that Russia's use of chemical agents on civilians to end a hostage crisis represents the responsibility of international organizations to draw lines in the sand regarding the development and use of incapacitating chemical agents (ICAs). If law enforcement is permitted such practices, then covert ICA development could lead to outright chemical warfare. Michael Crowley is Project Coordinator of the Bradford Non-Lethal Weapons Research Project at the University of Bradford. Malcolm Dando is Professor of International Security at the University of Bradford.

As you read, consider the following questions:

1. For what reason did Russian security forces use a secret ICA on civilians in 2002?
2. What effects do ICAs have on the body?
3. In what year did the CWC come into force?

O n October 26, 2002, to end a three-day siege on a theatre in Moscow by Chechen terrorists, Russian security forces used a

"Could Incapacitating Chemical Weapons Start an Arms Race?" by Michael Crowley and Malcolm Dando, *The Conversation*, October 24, 2014. https://theconversation.com/could-incapacitating-chemical-weapons-start-an-arms-race-33392 Licensed under CC BY 4.0 International

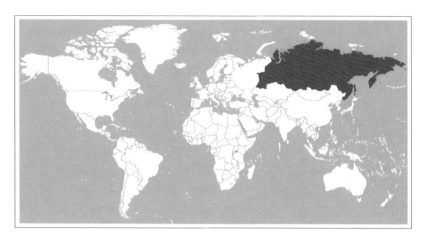

secret incapacitating chemical agent (ICA) weapon believed to affect the central nervous system. Although most of the 900 people being held hostage were freed, well over 100 of them were killed by the chemical agent; many more continue to suffer long-term health problems.

To this day, the Russian authorities refuse to disclose what weapon they used. Nor will they provide any details of the nature and levels of any incapacitating chemical weapons they may have developed or stockpiled.

But despite the official silence, a new report by the universities of Bradford and Bath documents evidence of continued Russian research into these chemical agents. That research includes computer modelling of "calmative gas" flows in enclosed spaces, as well as studies of the interaction of potential ICAs with human receptor sites.

And Russia is not alone; a number of other states have also conducted research that is potentially applicable to the study or development of ICA weapons. But the international community has turned a collective blind eye to such activities. Apparently, they consider the issue just too difficult to deal with.

The forthcoming Conference of the States Parties to the Chemical Weapons Convention in December 2014 will be a chance to rectify this omission before more countries become intrigued by these weapons—which would intensify the threat that they will proliferate and be dangerously misused.

Dangerous Stuff

There is no agreed definition of incapacitating chemical agents, but they can be described as a disparate range of substances—including pharmaceutical chemicals, bioregulators, and toxins—intended to act on the body's core biochemical and physiological systems to cause prolonged but non-permanent disability.

They include centrally acting agents, which produce loss of consciousness, sedation, hallucination, incoherence, disorientation, or paralysis. At inappropriate doses, death can result.

Proponents of these weapons have long promoted their development and use in law enforcement; they have also been pushed as a possible tool for military use, especially in locations where civilians and combatants are close together or intermingled.

In contrast, a broad range of observers, including scientific and medical organisations such as the British Medical Association, have pointed out that their production and use presents potentially grave dangers to human health and well-being.

ICA weapons can clearly be used for the purposes of torture and other human rights violations. If their development for law enforcement is tolerated, it could also become an excellent cover for covert offensive chemical weapons programmes, with the danger of further proliferation to both state and non-state actors. That slippery slope could ultimately lead to chemical warfare.

The new Bradford-Bath report examines contemporary research on a range of pharmaceutical chemicals potentially useful for the study or development of ICA weapons. As well as documenting research by Russian scientists, the report highlights the development and marketing by Chinese companies of ICA weapons employing an unknown anaesthetic agent for use against individuals, and the possession of such weapons in 2012 by the Chinese Peoples' Liberation Army.

The report highlights previous research into ICAs by Israel and the notorious use of an ICA weapon as an attempted assassination tool by Mossad on at least one occasion, in 1997. The more recent unconfirmed allegations of ICA weapons use by government forces during the ongoing Syrian civil war are also explored.

The report also highlights potentially relevant chemical and life science research conducted since 1997 in the Czech Republic, India, Iran, the United Kingdom and the United States.

Blurred Lines

ICA weapons clearly come under the scope of the Chemical Weapons Convention, which came into force in 1997 and which is monitored by the Organisation for the Prohibition of Chemical Weapons (OPCW). The use of any toxic chemicals as weapons in armed conflict is absolutely prohibited.

But there are differing interpretations as to whether such toxic chemicals may be employed for law enforcement purposes, and if so, in what circumstances and under what constraints. This ambiguity has never been satisfactorily addressed by the States that are party to the Convention; no OPCW policy-making organ has made any interpretative statements to clarify it.

That leaves CWC signatories to interpret the treaty and raises the risk that a "permissive" interpretation may evolve. And while various countries (including the UK and the US) have formally declared that they are not developing and do not possess ICA weapons, other states that have conducted ICA research remain silent.

If the OPCW does not act decisively to address the situation, more and more countries may start to harness advances in relevant scientific disciplines for ICA weapons development programs—or may be accused of doing so. And that, in turn, may encourage further states to conduct their own ICA weapons research and development programs—or even to start exploring an even broader range of chemical agents.

There is now a window of opportunity for states to halt the potential proliferation and misuse of these weapons. If they do not, we could face a new type of arms race, and perhaps the erosion of the prohibition on chemical weapons.

In Rhodesia and Syria Chemical and Biological Weapons Have Been Used Against Insurgents

Glenn Cross

In the following viewpoint, Glenn Cross argues that although there are norms and taboos governing the prohibition of chemical and biological weapons use, they have been ineffective. Cross outlines two specific examples, in the countries of Rhodesia (now Zimbabwe) and Syria, where these weapons have been, and are being used against internal insurgents. Following the viewpoint is a comparison of chemical and biological weapons. Cross is a member of the US Intelligence Community, and an expert on biological weapons; he is the author of "Dirty War: Rhodesia and Chemical, Biological Warfare."

As you read, consider the following questions:

1. As reported in the viewpoint, which country has used biological weapons since the end of World War II?
2. According to US intelligence as quoted by Cross, why is Syria using chemical weapons?
3. Why are norms that prohibit the use of chemical and biological weapons not very effective according to the author?

"Long Ignored: The Use of Chemical and Biological Weapons Against Insurgents," by Glenn Cross, War on The Rocks, August 15, 2017. Reprinted by permission.

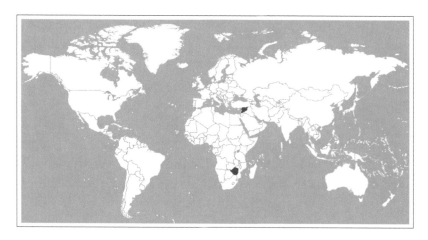

A conventional shibboleth is that chemical and biological agents have no place in modern conflicts. In this view, chemical and biological agents are not useful because they are inhumane, uncontrollable, ineffective, or obsolete in the face of modern conventional weapons. These arguments were put forth when the US decided to ban biological weapons, and later applied to chemical weapons. However, a review of chemical and biological weapons use since the end of World War I puts the lie to many of these claims. Chemical and biological agents possess significant utility in modern counterinsurgency campaigns, as Rhodesia and Syria have demonstrated. (One disclaimer is apropos at this point: This argument does not justify or condone the use of chemical or biological agents in any form or at any time unless legally sanctioned by the relevant international agreements.)

Throughout history, chemical and biological agents have demonstrated effectiveness against ill-equipped, ill-prepared, or poorly trained adversaries, especially insurgents. Examples of the use of these weapons against insurgents include Spain (Rif war, 1921–1927), Italy (1935–1936), Egypt (1963–1967), Rhodesia (mid–late 1970s), South Africa (1980s), Libya (1987), Iraq (1988), and Syria (2013–ongoing). And while the Spanish, Italian, Egyptian and Libyan uses are examples of the use of chemical weapons in inter-state conflict, most of the cases involve colonial governments using the weapons against native insurrections. The Rhodesian example illustrates a regime's largely internal use of chemical and biological agents against insurgents. These are clear parallels between this example and Syria's well-publicized use of chlorine and sarin against civilians, which has been ongoing since 2013.

As Chris Quillen points out, Arab nations used chemical weapons after conventional forces proved ineffective in the wake of prolonged conflict that strained economies, weakened international standing, and threatened vital assets. Quillen argues that chemical agents were used as a weapon of last resort and that therefore, these cases demonstrate the strength of the norms and taboos prohibiting the use of these weapons.

But a counterargument is that international norms are weakened with each consecutive use and the absence of an effective response. Richard Russell asserted in a 2005 article that "Nation-states are likely to learn from Saddam [Hussein] that chemical weapons are useful for waging war against nation-states ill-prepared to fight on a chemical battlefield as well as against internal insurgents and rebellious civilians."

The conclusion from these examples is that regimes in extremis—when the battle is for their very survival—seem to have little compunction about resorting to chemical and biological weapons use. The much-heralded international norms and conventions prohibiting and condemning chemical and biological development and use go out the window when a regime's survival is at stake. In academic and policy circles, the norms against chemical and biological development and use seem almost sacrosanct, inviolable. The Rhodesian case dispels the myth and offers a more nuanced understanding of the role the norms play and the circumstances in which those norms are abandoned. When regimes are fighting for survival and perceive that chemical or biological agents can help defeat an insurgency, the use of these weapons becomes more attractive despite the existence of norms. The examples of Rhodesia and Syria show that the international community must be united and demonstrate the requisite political will to enforce norms if the use of chemical and biological weapons is to be prevented.

The Rhodesian Case Study

The Rhodesian example is likely the only example of biological weapons use by a nation since the end of World War II. The case allows us to examine the rationale behind a decision not only to develop, but also to use, biological weapons agents. Rhodesia also sheds light on other post-World War II chemical weapons cases, such as Iraq's, particularly against its Kurdish population, and Syria's, against insurgents in its civil war.

The lesson of Rhodesia and Syria is that regimes are much more likely to use these unconventional agents against internal opposition (i.e., insurgents and rebellious populations) than against foreign state adversaries. The Rhodesian case demonstrates how a small, internationally isolated regime can develop effective chemical and biological agents undetected and use those agents with lethal effect against both internal and external guerrilla threats.

Rhodesia covertly established a rudimentary, small-scale chemical and biological program using readily available materials, equipment, and techniques. Starting in 1965, Rhodesia faced international sanctions and a blockade of supplies entering the country through Mozambique's port of Beira. Salisbury, [the capital city of Rhodesia,] depended on Portugal (until the 1974 coup) and South Africa for foreign support (which became increasingly sporadic after 1975). The loss of Portuguese support and the unpredictability of South African assistance led Rhodesia to turn to chemical and biological weapons as self-help.

Rhodesian decision-makers adopted an unconventional response to the growing imbalance that favored the far more numerous insurgents. After the collapse of Portuguese colonial power in Mozambique—along with the dramatic increase in guerrilla recruitments and the escalating violence—people within the security structure realized the counterinsurgency could not be won solely through the conventional military.

With scant material resources, the project employed relative novices in basic facilities to produce significant amounts of lethal material in a short period of time. The Rhodesian effort also shows that states, groups, or individuals lacking funds or sophisticated equipment can easily use toxic agricultural and industrial chemicals as chemical weapons agents. By minimizing reliance on foreign suppliers and limiting personnel to a small, tightly knit group, nations and non-state actors can reduce the likelihood of discovery by foreign intelligence services.

If the Rhodesian sources are credible, their chemical and biological effort at times inflicted more guerrilla casualties than the conventional military operations did. This comparative success was largely due to guerrilla hit-and-run tactics that emphasized avoiding contact with Rhodesian forces in favor of attacking softer civilian targets. In other words, where the Rhodesian military struggled to locate and engage an elusive foe, the chemical and biological effort sought to kill the guerrillas in their camps and bases, and among their village supporters. These attributes made chemical and biological warfare well-suited to counterinsurgency when the regime's aim was survival.

The lessons of the Rhodesian chemical and biological program and its legacy are more relevant today than is commonly realized. Outside the international system—and already under crushing sanctions—Rhodesia had very little to lose in adopting chemical and biological agents. International opprobrium would have had little effect on Rhodesian decision-making. Second, little global attention was focused on events inside Rhodesia. What little attention Rhodesia did get myopically monitored Soviet and Chinese support for the insurgent parties, who were widely seen as Marxist proxies. The covert nature of the Rhodesian program compounded the lack of attention. Western diplomatic, intelligence, and journalistic channels did not report the Rhodesian production and use of chemical and biological agents, despite ineffective insurgent efforts to raise awareness of the issue.

The Difference between Chemical Weapons and Biological Weapons

Key Difference: A chemical weapon is any weapon that uses a man-made chemical to kill people. On the other hand, a biological weapon uses a bacteria or virus, or in some cases poison that comes directly from bacteria to kill people.

Chemical weapons and biological weapons are two of the most devastating and calamitous weapons. These are such kinds of weapons which are very harmful to [the] human population.

A chemical weapon is any weapon that uses a man-made chemical to kill people. Chemical weapons can be widely discrete in a solid, liquid and gaseous form. It is the effortless way for subversives to kill people. For the last so many years, these chemical weapons are used all over the world. However, it has been decided for chemical weapons to be eliminated from the face of the planet. Chemical weapons were never used in ancient times, as they didn't have the technology. If the chemical weapon is placed ideally, it can kill 100 to 1000 times less people as compared to one biological weapon of the same weight. According to howstuffworks.com, "In World War I, the German army released tons of the gas to create a cloud that the wind carried toward the enemy."

Biological weapons are actual living organisms like a virus. They are slower acting, spreading a disease such as anthrax or smallpox through a population before the first signs are noticed. If you were to dump a load of human waste into a town's well, that would be a simple form of biological warfare; human and animal waste contain bacteria that are deadly in a variety of ways.

Biological weapons are less mass-destructive, but more dangerous. Biological representatives are living organisms that have a spiteful habit of spreading from host to host. They're the gift that keeps on giving. Plus, symptoms take time to manifest. Deadly disease may have spread before anyone's aware an attack has occurred.

"Difference between Chemical Weapons and Biological Weapons," www.differencebetween.info.

International norms against chemical and biological weapons had no impact on Rhodesia's decision to use these agents. Although the regime was aware of treaty obligations, no evidence exists to suggest that Rhodesian authorities even debated the reaction of the international community when they established their chemical and biological weapons effort. As a footnote, the British government deposited a reservation to the Biological Weapons and Toxins Convention in March 1975 stating that the UK could not be held liable for any breach of the convention that might occur in Rhodesia while the colony remained beyond British control. The Soviet Union promptly protested the British reservation. Clearly, authorities in London wanted to avoid blame for any Rhodesian violations of the Biological Weapons and Toxins Convention, while Moscow sought to hold the UK culpable for acts by the rebellious Rhodesians. In either case, the outlaw Rhodesians actually involved in biological weapons use were beyond the pale of international obligation. The Rhodesians believed using these agents against the counterinsurgency was necessary to preserve their regime and way of life regardless of international law.

The Syrian Example

Like the Iraqi chemical weapons program, Syria's interest in chemical weapons began after the Egyptian use in Yemen in the 1960s. However, Damascus did not adopt a full-fledged chemical weapons program until its military inferiority was unmasked by the 1982 Israeli invasion of Lebanon. The sense of inferiority—and the perceived unwillingness of Arab neighbors to rise to Syria's aid—resulted in Damascus's adoption of chemical weapons by the mid-1980s. Chemical weapons were the most expedient means of protecting the Assad regime from catastrophic defeat at Israeli hands. Similarly, the Rhodesian chemical and biological effort began out of an increasing awareness of the deteriorating security situation in the face of international isolation.

Even though Damascus's interest in chemical weapons first arose in an international/regional context focused on deterring

Israel, the utility of the weapons for the Syrian regime has been, like Rhodesia, in countering its internal insurgency. The Syrian attack on Khan Sheikhoun demonstrates the utility of chemical weapons in the counterinsurgency. According to the declassified assessment by the US intelligence community, released on April 11, 2017:

> The Syrian regime maintains the capability and intent to use chemical weapons against the opposition to prevent the loss of territory deemed critical to its survival. We assess that Damascus launched this chemical attack in response to an opposition offensive in northern Hamah Province that threatened key infrastructure.

On the same day, a senior US official elaborated on the threat posed by the rebel offensive in Hamah. The official stated:

> The regime we think calculated that with its manpower spread quite thin, trying to support both defensive operations and consolidation operations in Aleppo and along that north-south spine of western Syria, and also trying to support operations which required it to send manpower and resources east toward Palmyra, we believe that the regime probably calculated at that point that chemical weapons were necessary in order to try to make up for the manpower deficiency.

These assessments clearly illustrate that Damascus resorted to the use of chemical weapons to compensate for inadequate conventional military resources as it sought to counter an imminent threat to a key population center and a vital air base. The US intelligence assessment even emphasized these regime assets as "critical to its survival."

Effective Constraints on Chemical and Biological Use

Although a prevailing assumption has held that chemical and biological weapons will not be used because of a combination of ineffectiveness, international norms, and international agreements, Rhodesia and Syria show that this perspective doesn't tell the full story. Deterrence (i.e., the credible threat of military action) likely is the only effective means of preventing the use of these weapons. International agreements and prohibitive international norms or taboos are largely ineffective unless the political will exists to punish the transgressor. Prohibitions against chemical and biological weapons are enshrined in international agreements, most notably the Biological Weapons and Toxins Convention and the Chemical Weapons Convention. Yet these agreements have been ineffective in constraining the production and use of these agents.

The political will for action in the international community has also long been severely lacking—witness the inaction after the gassing in Halabja and President Obama's "red line" in Syria. After the Obama administration ultimately decided against striking Syria in 2013, the Kerry-Lavrov agreement resulted in Damascus's accession to the Chemical Weapon Convention and its surrender of declared chemical weapons stocks for destruction. Yet as later events demonstrated, Syria retained chemical weapons materials and remained willing to use them against civilians, making the ultimate value of the Kerry-Lavrov agreement questionable.

Despite the conventions, several state parties to these agreements likely have chemical and/or biological weapons programs. A number of states have maintained biological weapons programs in contravention to the Biological Weapons Convention, as demonstrated by the well-known example of Yeltsin's termination of the Soviet program in 1992. Another party to the convention, South Africa, developed and used biological weapons agents for over a decade after ratifying the agreement. Although the Chemical Weapons Convention now has been in force for 20 years, several signatories likely still possess chemical weapons. According to a June 2017 fact sheet assembled by the Arms Control Association, convention signatories thought to possibly retain covert chemical agents or munitions include China, Iran, Israel, North Korea, Russia, and Syria.

The apparent lack of international political will to confront the use of chemical and biological weapons should be evidence that the norms and taboos against the production, possession, and use of these weapons have eroded. Those norms and taboos represent the prevailing international consensus—embodied in international agreements—that underpins the political will to action. Norms represent a consensus defining appropriate and inappropriate conduct by nation-states under anarchic conditions. Norms are not universal nor are they immutable.

Taboos, on the other hand, are prohibitions on conduct considered so morally repugnant and reprehensible so as to be universally condemned. Following the experiences of World War I, chemical and biological weapons became taboo. But even so, World War II saw a massive increase in the number of national chemical and biological programs. Arguably, Allied and Axis powers were deterred from using these weapons by fear of retaliation from the opposing side.

Yet the Axis powers used chemical and biological agents on an enormous scale against vulnerable populations. Japanese units using weapons developed by Unit 731 wrought untold destruction on Chinese military units and civilian communities. For his part, Adolf Hitler may have prohibited use of chemical and biological agents against Allied forces, yet he was not dissuaded from using poison gas (Zyklon B) against millions of civilians. In neither of these instances was the taboo effective. The effect of deterrence and the relevance of international norms in preventing chemical and biological weapons use is arguably lessened when a nation-state is facing an ill-prepared or vulnerable population. The Arab, Rhodesian, and South African cases all bear this out.

Syria's recent use of chemical weapons likely has diminished effectiveness of the chemical and biological prohibitions, as have previous uses (i.e., Egypt, Libya, and Iraq). The international community's failure to act more decisively may embolden other marginal nations to explore chemical and biological adoption and use to counter threats to their internal security.

Although the US cruise missile strike on April 6, 2017, against Syria's Shayrat airfield signalled Washington's resolve to punish

Damascus for future chemical weapons use, the political impact (and legality) of the US strike remains debatable, especially given allegations of continued Syrian use. According to an article in the German paper *Die Welt* in July 2017, "Western intelligence agencies confirmed to *Die Welt* that Syria's government continues to use poison gas against its own population. Apparently, the regime understands the latest signals from the US as an encouragement." As of early June 2017, the US government itself warned of a possibly imminent Syria chemical weapons attack, further suggesting the attack on Shayrat failed to sufficiently punish the Assad regime.

One reason the US strike may not have prevented further use is that it came from the US alone. Unilateral action against the transgressor demonstrated the weakness of the norm in that the international community lacked the political will to act. The absence of political will is highlighted by Russia's repeated vetoes of UN resolutions condemning Syria for its chemical weapons use. Furthermore, a member of the UN's war crimes commission, Carla Del Ponte, resigned in early August 2017, saying, "The Assad government has perpetrated horrible crimes against humanity and used chemical weapons … I am quitting this commission, which is not backed by any political will. I have no power as long as the [UN] Security Council does nothing. There is no justice for Syria."

The Bottom Line

Despite the international moratorium on chemical weapons use in interstate conflict, these agents are effective in suppressing internal violence. Chemical and biological weapons' lack of utility against well-prepared, well-equipped adversaries deters their use against modern militaries, yet historically the weapons have been effective against the unprepared or vulnerable.

The post-World War II examples of chemical weapons use show that their greatest utility is in intrastate counterinsurgency operations and in attacks on ill-prepared and poorly equipped or trained adversaries. This perceived advantage is likely the greatest obstacle to the elimination of these arms from national arsenals.

As demonstrated in Rhodesia, Iraq, and Syria, the norm against chemical and biological weapons use is weakest in low-intensity counterinsurgencies involving rogue or pariah regimes, and when poisons and toxins are used in special operations and assassinations (examples include Chile under Pinochet, South Africa, and Russia). The Rhodesian and Syrian cases clearly show the relative inability of international norms to prevent the use of chemical and biological weapons in these cases. For norms to be truly effective, there must be unanimity among nations about enforcing the prohibitions. As we've seen in Syria, such consensus is elusive, and the international community has failed to act. As a consequence, the world faces a sad, but inevitable conclusion. The Syrian regime is unlikely to ever face justice for its use of chemical weapons.

In Iran and Iraq Researchers Seek to Help Chemical Warfare Victims

Richard Stone

In the following viewpoint, Richard Stone analyzes the research being conducted on the victims of chemical weapons from the Iran-Iraq War. Stone's reporting outlines efforts being taken in several countries to first understand the complicated set of adverse reactions to the chemicals and then to administer medications thought to help the victims. An award-winning science writer, Stone is the senior science editor at the Howard Hughes Medical Institute.

As you read, consider the following questions:

1. Which Arab country is responsible for the majority of chemical attacks reported by the viewpoint?
2. Which body organ is most affected by the mustard chemical according to Stone?
3. According to the author, what is the living memorial to Iran's chemical weapons victims?

O n a chilly morning in September 1987, in the waning days of the Iran-Iraq War, an 18-year-old Iranian soldier named Seyed Naser Emadi drove from a battlefield in northwestern Iran to a hospital in Nagadeh, a city a couple hours away. Crammed in the back of his Land Rover were four soldiers, moaning, vomiting, and

"Seeking Answers for Iran's Chemical Weapons Victims—Before Time Runs Out," by Richard Stone, American Association for the Advancement of Science, January 4, 2018. Reprinted by permission.

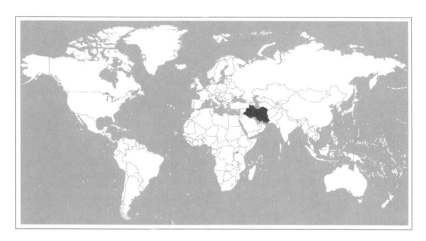

coughing. "I'll never forget the sound of their breathing," Emadi says. "It was rattling, raspy." The terrified young men did not know what was happening, and Emadi had no idea how to help them.

They complained about the cold, so Emadi rolled up his window. The air in the vehicle became stifling, and a strong chemical odor wafted from the men's uniforms. Emadi grew nauseous and dizzy, but he made it to the hospital. There, he tried to rouse the nearest victim, whose face and hands had large blisters. The young man would not wake up. As Emadi and a hospital aide carried the victim out of the vehicle, a blister on the man's arm burst, and fluid splattered on the back of Emadi's hand. A couple hours later, he felt a burning sensation and his own hand began to blister.

The experience set Emadi on the path to becoming a medical researcher. (He is now a dermatologist at Tehran University of Medical Sciences and a volunteer with Doctors Without Borders.) It also highlighted one of the cruelest practices in the 1980–1988 conflict, which also featured child soldiers and trench warfare. For the first time ever on a battlefield, nerve agents including sarin and tabun were unleashed by Iraqi forces. "These are the most toxic chemical warfare agents ever developed," says Jonathan Newmark, a neurologist in Burke, Virginia, who has helped develop countermeasures against such weapons at the US Army Medical Research Institute of Chemical Defense (USAMRICD) in Edgewood, Maryland, and other agencies. And on scores of occasions, Iraq shelled soldiers and villagers with sulfur mustard—the chemical that afflicted Emadi and his passengers.

After the war, Iraq—pressured to own up to the attacks—acknowledged that it had "consumed" 1800 tons of mustard, 600 tons of sarin, and 140 tons of tabun. All told, according to Iran's Foundation of Martyrs and Veterans Affairs (FMVA), the chemical onslaught killed nearly 5000 Iranians and sickened more than 100,000. That doesn't include Iraqi victims: In March 1988, Iraq's forces attacked its own citizens with mustard and nerve agents in Halabja, killing as many as 5000 and wounding 7000.

Sulfur mustard, a family of compounds first used in World War I, left the deepest and most visible scars on survivors of the war. Three decades later, about 56,000 Iranians are coping with lingering health effects from the blistering agent, ranging from skin lesions and failing corneas to chronic obstructive lung disease and possibly cancer, says Tooba Ghazanfari, an immunologist at Shahed University here.

The scale of the atrocities means that Iran has a unique opportunity to study the long-term effects of chemical weapons. Ghazanfari is leading an effort at a dozen research centers across Iran to uncover how wartime mustard exposures wreaked molecular mayhem that, decades later, triggers illnesses and death. "I'm pretty amazed about the scale of exposures and how many people have been followed," says neuroscientist David Jett, director of the Countermeasures Against Chemical Threats (CounterACT) Program at the US National Institutes of Health in Bethesda, Maryland, which is spearheading R&D on several promising methods of neutralizing such agents.

The data, some of which are beginning to appear in Western journals, have unavoidable limitations. The Iranian researchers can only estimate the doses that victims absorbed, and complicating the picture is the fact that Iraqi forces sometimes attacked with mustard and nerve agents simultaneously. "That makes it really difficult to determine what's going on," says James Madsen, a physician and lead clinical consultant in USAMRICD's Chemical Casualty Care Division. Still, US researchers say the Iranian findings are pointing to new molecular targets for treating mustard's long-term effects.

So far, Iran has not undertaken a similar study of nerve agent survivors, who also number in the thousands. Based on Japanese victims of sarin attacks by the Aum Shinrikyo doomsday cult in the mid-1990s and US soldiers possibly exposed to sarin in Iraq, researchers suspect that nerve agents leave a legacy of neurological damage. But chemical weapons experts have struggled to link sarin to specific chronic symptoms; they are hoping for some clarity from a US review that is about to be released. And Iranian researchers say they may start their own probe of nerve agents' long-term health effects. "We want to get the knowledge out," says Mohammad-Reza Soroush, a physician here at the Janbazan Medical and Engineering Research Center.

With his bearish frame and thick black beard, Ali Cherchi would be an imposing figure—if he weren't propped up in a hospital bed with an oxygen tube in his nose and an intravenous line plying him with antibiotics. His infection-riddled lungs are giving out.

Like many teenage boys filled with patriotic fervor during the war, Cherchi lied about his age, saying he was 18 instead of 17 so he could enlist in the army. One day in 1986, near the Persian Gulf in southern Iran, the Iraqis shelled his 200-strong platoon with mustard and tabun. Many of the young men had beards, so their gas masks did not fit tightly. "I felt like I was suffocating," Cherchi says. Only a few dozen survived the attack, and since then most of the rest have died. "I'm the champion for having lasted so long," he says with an ironic laugh.

For years, Cherchi indeed considered himself fortunate: He studied law, married, and had children. But now, a short stroll can leave him gasping for breath. Lung infections land him for weeks at a stretch here at Sasan Hospital, Iran's premier facility for chemical weapons victims, which treats as many as 150 such patients on any given day. As Cherchi tells his life story in a hospital ward, his confident voice falters and, eyes widening, he reaches for an inhaler. "Chemical weapons are not fair," he says.

An old scourge ruined Cherchi's lungs. Called mustard because of its odor and the enormous yellowish blisters, or bullae, that it forms on the skin, bis(2-chloroethyl) sulfide—the primary member of a family of noxious compounds—debuted on the battlefield in July 1917, when Germany used it against UK and Canadian soldiers near Ypres, Belgium. After a mustard-filled artillery shell detonates, the chemical is dispersed as fine droplets that settle to the ground. In hot and dry climates, mustard can vaporize and is more likely to be inhaled. A mere 7 grams—a teaspoonful—is a lethal dose, Madsen says.

How the mustards produce their acute effects is well known. The oily liquid dissolves readily in fat, allowing it to penetrate skin. Inside cells, the chemical corrupts DNA and proteins. Recovery from the tissue damage can take months, and some World War I mustard survivors succumbed years later to respiratory failure.

Countries stockpiled sulfur mustard during World War II, but it saw limited use in battle. However, thousands of workers in a weapons factory on Ōkunoshima, an island in Japan, were exposed to mustard on the job. Studies flagged an elevated lung cancer risk, but failed to shed light on the mechanism of sulfur mustard's long-term effects, says pharmacologist Jeffrey Laskin, who directs a CounterACT center on chemical weapons countermeasures at Rutgers University's Robert Wood Johnson Medical School in Piscataway, New Jersey.

Iranian scientists are seeking answers. A decade ago, Ghazanfari and colleagues launched the Sardasht-Iran cohort study, named after a town in the northwest part of the country that was the site of one of the war's more reprehensible acts.

On 28 June 1987, Iraqi aircraft dropped four 250-kilogram bombs filled with mustard on residential areas of Sardasht. "It was a completely innocent city," says Mohammad-Reza Vaez Mahdavi, a Shahed University physiologist who studies the survivors. Records show that 8025 of the 12,000-odd residents were exposed. A few dozen—mostly children and elderly—died within hours or days. About 1500 people suffered moderate to severe symptoms, and at least 100 have since succumbed to respiratory failure, Ghazanfari says.

With funding from FMVA, Ghazanfari's team is tracking the health of 850 male victims, now aged 30 to 70. Most still reside in Sardasht. For a control group, the scientists recruited 150 men of equivalent age in Rabat, a village 15 kilometers from Sardasht. During the war, Rabat was shelled often—but never with chemical weapons. "Both populations endured a lot of stress," Ghazanfari says. In principle, that allows her team to zero in on illnesses in Sardasht that can't be chalked up to stress or factors such as diet and economic status, which are similar in Sardasht and Rabat.

The Sardasht survivors have much higher rates of eye and skin disorders. A few have also developed cutaneous T-cell lymphoma at the site of old mustard burns. Emadi says the uncommon skin cancer may also explain mysterious lesions that doctors in the early 20th century noted in World War I mustard victims. But he says that benign skin lesions are far more common in the victims: patches that lack sweat glands or the ability to secrete sebum, resulting in intensely itchy, dry skin that's susceptible to infection.

It's in the lungs where mustard wreaks the most havoc. "Many soldiers on the battlefield don't have symptoms, but years later they come to us with problems," says Mostafa Ghanei, a physician at Baqiyatallah University of Medical Sciences here who consults for the Organisation for the Prohibition of Chemical Weapons (OPCW) in The Hague, Netherlands. Mustard creates what he calls a "unique pathology": peribronchial fibrosis—a thickening in tissues surrounding the bronchi—coupled with an airway obstruction called bronchiolitis obliterans.

To get at the roots of these symptoms, the Iranian team is probing a complex cascade of biochemical perturbations that persists in mustard survivors. They have detected, for example, revved up signaling molecules involved in inflammation, such as tumor necrosis factor α (TNFα) and other cytokines; skewed populations of natural killer cells and other immune cells; imbalances in the protein-destroying enzymes called proteases; and a shortening of the telomeres, the "end caps" on chromosomes, which indicates prematurely aged cells.

"They're doing a really good job documenting what's going on," Laskin says. But why the cellular dysfunction occurs decades after exposure is still a puzzle, he adds.

DNA methylation and other epigenetic alterations—chemical changes to DNA that can alter a gene's expression without affecting its protein-coding sequence—may underlie some of the lasting biochemical havoc, Ghanei says. He and colleagues have found evidence, for example, that methylation of tumor suppressor genes may inactivate them and help explain the development of peribronchial fibrosis as well as slightly elevated rates of certain cancers, in particular blood cancers.

In the past, Ghanei says, mustard victims with chronic symptoms were given standard treatments for chronic pulmonary disorders such as asthma: corticosteroids to tamp down inflammation and β2-agonists for smooth muscle relaxation. He and his colleagues now view oxidative stress as a prime target, because levels of an important antioxidant and an enzyme that scavenges destructive free radicals are suppressed in mustard victims. Iranian doctors now treat chronic mustard patients with antioxidants such as N-acetylcysteine, which alleviates the frequency and severity of bronchiolitis attacks, Ghanei has found.

Researchers in the United States are exploring other potential treatments. Drugs that neutralize TNFα might help, Laskin says. Another promising lead came when pediatric pulmonologist Livia Veress of the University of Colorado in Denver and colleagues zeroed in on fibrin clots in rats exposed to mustard. When she dissected the animals, she pulled out of their lungs white clots called casts that looked like "tree branches," she says. "I realized I'd seen that before"—in children with plastic bronchitis, a rare complication of surgery to repair congenital heart defects. Veress tested a clot-busting drug, tissue plasminogen activator (tPA), in rats exposed to normally lethal mustard doses—they all survived. Her team has since given tPA to seven children with plastic bronchitis, which normally has a mortality rate of up to 60%. "These are really sick kids," she says. All survived; other hospitals have treated 22 children, all of whom recovered, too. "It's pretty darn cool," Veress says. Her team is working toward US Food and Drug Administration (FDA) approval for tPA's use for plastic bronchitis and next month, they will start testing the drug in pigs to further demonstrate its potential as a sulfur mustard treatment.

Those prospects, although tantalizing, are still on the horizon, and mustard remains a grave concern: In March 2016, the Islamic State group shelled a village in Iraq near Kirkuk with rockets filled with mustard. "It is just as much of a threat now as it was in the Iran-Iraq War," Madsen says.

That is equally true for the nerve agents, which many nations still stockpile and which were used as recently as last April against civilians and rebel soldiers in Syria.

Syed Abbas Foroutan remembers their grim debut. In March 1984, he was a young army doctor running a unit for treating mustard victims when some soldiers with unusual symptoms were brought in. They were coughing and short of breath, and some were vomiting and drifting in and out of consciousness. It was clear to the doctors that they weren't dealing with mustard. "We could only say it was not this, not that," Foroutan says—until he found a symptom common to all the victims: "Their pupils were constricted to pinholes."

That pointed to a nerve agent. Such weapons form a covalent bond to and inactivate acetylcholinesterase (AChE), an enzyme that breaks down acetylcholine in synapses, thereby regulating levels of the neurotransmitter. A few days later, comatose victims started arriving to the clinic. Foroutan checked their AChE levels—they were near zero. The clincher was that the ill soldiers responded to atropine, which binds to and blocks acetylcholine receptors, reducing the effects of excess levels of the neurotransmitter. That realization was the beginning of a grave challenge for a young doctor fresh out of medical school, says Newmark, who has studied Foroutan's experiences. "He was the world's first physician to care for battlefield nerve agent casualties."

Undeterred by charges that it was engaging in a war crime, Iraq repeatedly shelled Iranian forces with tabun, and later with sarin as well as a binary form of the agent, cyclosarin. As Iraqi chemists learned to synthesize nerve agents with fewer contaminants and the military became more adroit at delivering them, the attacks were deadlier. Some casualties went "from fully functioning to seizing and comatose in seconds," Newmark says. Emadi, who witnessed such deaths, calls the victims "chemical martyrs."

To cope with the more potent threat, Foroutan pumped afflicted patients with massive doses of atropine—up to 10 times the amount that the United States and the North Atlantic Treaty Organization advise, near the threshold where the drug itself becomes toxic. "Foroutan was doing the best he could with what he had," Madsen says.

The radical treatment paid off, Newmark says. In most nerve agent fatalities, death occurs after the agent binds to enough AChE to block signal transmission from the brain's respiratory center to the diaphragm, paralyzing the muscle that's vital for breathing. "It takes fairly high doses of atropine to get into the brain," Madsen says. "What Foroutan did was intuitive. He gave so much atropine, we think that it started to take care of the [central nervous system] effects." Newmark puts it this way: "If a soldier got a snoot full of nerve agent, he was lucky to get to Foroutan's unit."

But what happened in later years to Foroutan's patients—and to thousands of others who survived nerve agent attacks—is largely unknown. That frustrates researchers, who would like to follow up on hints that exposure takes a long-term toll.

One clue comes from an episode in the United States, during Prohibition, when doctors in New York City and elsewhere in the 1920s, started seeing patients with muscle spasms, tingling and numbness in the legs, and, in some cases, paralysis. Medical sleuths eventually zeroed in on the cause: an adulterant, triorthocresyl phosphate, in a bootleg ginger liquor. That compound, like nerve agents, is an organophosphate, and the symptoms that afflicted the "Ginger Jake" drinkers—some 30,000 documented cases—are now known as organophosphate-induced delayed neurotoxicity (OPIDN). The same syndrome affected one victim of the Aum Shinrikyo cult's sarin terrorism, says Bahie Abou-Donia, a neurobiologist at Duke University in Durham, North Carolina. "It would not surprise me to see OPIDN in the Iranian survivors," Madsen says.

There's firmer evidence, he says, that nerve agents mess with the mind. Studies of the Aum Shinrikyo survivors link exposure "even at really low doses" to symptoms such as nightmares, headaches, drowsiness, confusion, memory deficits, irritability, and depression—a syndrome called organophosphorus-ester-induced chronic neurotoxicity (OPICN). In March 1991, during the Gulf War, tens of thousands of US soldiers may have been exposed to low doses of sarin after the destruction of an Iraqi ammunition dump, says Abou-Donia, a sarin expert. An unknown percentage of cases of the still-controversial Gulf War Syndrome, he says, may in fact be OPICN.

More clarity on the long-term effects of nerve agents will come from a US National Toxicology Program report on sarin. The draft review concludes that sarin's chronic effects include AChE inhibition, vision and memory problems in people, as well as nerve pathology detailed in animal studies.

The Iranian veterans could yield a more definitive picture. "Whatever comes out of Iran on this," Newmark says, "will be the best human data that exists." But so far, no one is gathering it. After the war, Foroutan became a professor—he's now at Shahid Beheshti University of Medical Sciences here—and has not tracked his former patients. And zeroing in on late nerve agent effects is not simple. "We don't have reliable information on who was exposed solely to nerve agents," says Janbazan medical researcher Batool Mousavi, because of the Iraqi practice of bombarding troops with nerve agents and mustard simultaneously or on consecutive days.

Foroutan believes that it's not too late to delve into the long-term consequences. "We need a Sardasht cohort for nerve cases," he says. It could even be an international effort, Newmark suggests, if Iran were to set up a collaboration under OPCW's auspices. "It's important to know if neuropathology and resultant long-term effects actually occur in humans," Jett adds, "before we approach the FDA for approval of a neuroprotectant drug."

In the heart of Tehran, a modest one-story building is a living memorial to Iran's chemical weapons victims. Inside the Tehran Peace Museum, exhibits recount the global history of chemical warfare. Chemical victims of the Iran-Iraq War volunteer as docents. One is named Ali Reza Yazdanpanah.

When he was 15 years old, Yazdanpanah tricked his mother into signing his enlistment papers. Several weeks later, he and 31 other young men in his regiment were exposed to mustard near Khorramshahr, a port city on the Persian Gulf, near the Iraq border. Some of the blistering agent got in his eyes. "I lost my sight for some time," he says. It came back, but he has had to endure four cornea transplantations, and is on a waiting list for a new pair of lungs. He says he has never felt completely well.

Yazdanpanah is keeping the memory alive. And as a subject in Iran's research efforts, he hopes his experience will benefit future victims of these ghoulish weapons. "The best years of my life," he says, "were stolen from me."

In the United States Experts Raise Concerns About Biowarfare

Margaret Steen

In the following viewpoint, Margaret Steen analyzes whether the United States is properly prepared to deal with a chemical or biological weapons attack. Steen provides a list of the biological agents of possible concern and details how the US can become properly prepared to weather an attack. Margaret Steen is a contributing writer for Emergency Management *magazine.*

As you read, consider the following questions:

1. What are the six agents that may be used in an attack according to the viewpoint?
2. What two events caused the United States to begin preparing for a chemical or biological attack?
3. According to Steen, what are the three possible causes of infectious diseases?

I s the United States dangerously complacent about possible biological and chemical weapon attacks, leaving open the possibility of mass deaths or a huge disruption in the economy or both? Or has the country in fact come a long way in its preparations to protect itself against this type of attack?

The answer may be both.

"Are We Ready for Biological and Chemical Attacks?" by Margaret Steen, Emergency Management, October 29, 2015. Reprinted by permission.

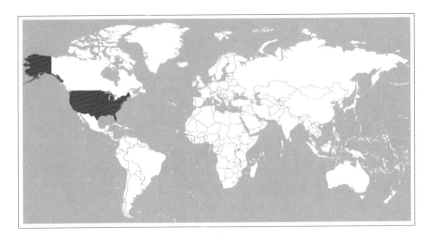

Tom Ridge, former Homeland Security secretary, and Joe Lieberman, former senator, are co-chairing a Blue Ribbon Study Panel on Biodefense hosted by Hudson Institute and the Inter-University Center for Terrorism Studies. They wrote in *Roll Call* that "our nation is dangerously unprepared to prevent or respond to" attacks with biological and chemical weapons, citing recent cuts in funding for readiness efforts.

The Gravest Dangers

The list of agents that officials and experts worry about most "is populated by bacteria and viruses that have found their way into state weapons programs," said Rocco Casagrande, managing director of Gryphon Scientific in Takoma Park, Md. These are agents that could be disseminated to thousands of people—for example, with an aerosol attack or through the food supply. Here's a summary of some of the agents that cause the most concern:

- Anthrax: This causes a bacterial infection and is cause for concern because it has been successfully intentionally released. It doesn't spread from person to person, but the spores are hardy and can be dispersed over a wide area.
- Smallpox: This virus was declared eradicated in 1980 and currently exists in two labs, one in the United States and

one in Russia. Because people are no longer routinely vaccinated for it, an outbreak—whether caused intentionally or accidentally—could be devastating. The United States stockpiles smallpox vaccine for use in an emergency.

- Plague: This bacterial infection was the cause of the Black Death in the 14th century and has been used in warfare. It is also endemic in the Southwest United States—two visitors to Yosemite National Park in California are suspected to have contracted it this year, for example. It can be treated with antibiotics, reducing the death rate.

- Tularemia: Also called rabbit fever, this bacterial infection is acquired from rabbits or ticks. There are about 100 cases per year in the US. There is no vaccine for it, but antibiotics can treat it.

- Viral hemorrhagic fevers: This category includes Ebola. The recent Ebola outbreak, even though it did not involve terrorism, illustrates the level of alarm and social disruption that could come from an outbreak. However, these illnesses are difficult to weaponize.

- Botulism: Botulism exists in improperly preserved foods and can be treated with an antitoxin.

They discussed the recent Ebola outbreak, which "spread because we and the rest of the world did not manage the disease properly"—and ask what would happen if an infectious agent were deliberately released.

Taking a longer view, however, experts say the United States has indeed made progress.

"I think we've come a huge way," said Rocco Casagrande, managing director of Gryphon Scientific in Takoma Park, Md. The group provides analysis of prevention and response to chemical, biological and nuclear attacks. "Prior to 1997, there was almost no effort put into this at the state and local level. Not many jurisdictions were taking it seriously."

The terrorist attacks of 9/11, followed by the mailing of anthrax that fall, focused a lot of attention and money on how to prevent, prepare for and recover from such an attack.

Bioterrorism has not always been part of the curriculum in medical school, for example, but is now included in textbooks on infectious diseases, said Dr. Robert J. Leggiadro, an adjunct professor of biology at Villanova University and board-certified physician in pediatrics and pediatric infectious diseases.

However, Casagrande agrees that funding has gotten less secure and the focus has waned in recent years, especially on the public health side. (Law enforcement, he said, is still working on preventing attacks.)

"I worry that a lot of that initial energy and emphasis has waned," Casagrande said. "A lot of places are losing focus. Equipment is getting old, consumables are reaching their shelf life, and plans have gone unexercised in a lot of cases."

As years pass without major attacks, attention—and funding—gets redirected.

"People are very excited about these events when they occur, and then it's no longer in the news, and other issues come up," said William Karesh, executive vice president for health and policy at the EcoHealth Alliance, a nonprofit science-based health and conservation organization. His work focuses on the links between ecology and health. "The emphasis and funding and pressure to do something go away."

People sometimes point to problems in how a small-scale problem was handled—for example, a person who returns from traveling with a contagious illness—and assume this means the government is unprepared for a major outbreak.

But "[a] lot more systems would be engaged if it was super-serious," Casagrande said. For example, he said, recognizing an unusual illness if there are just a few cases—and determining whether it's the result of an attack or naturally occurring—is "really, really difficult." But in a large-scale attack, there could be dozens or even hundreds of people affected at once. "It would be hard to miss that, as opposed to just one guy showing up at one hospital."

One of the issues is that many of the agents, such as anthrax or plague that could be used for a biological attack, also exist in the environment. The first step, Leggiadro said, is to diagnose the disease. A diagnosis of smallpox, which does not exist outside of labs, would be an "international emergency," he said. "For the others, you need to figure out if there's a benign cause."

Karesh, who does a lot of work with emerging infectious diseases, especially their links to wildlife, said understanding disease hot spots can help authorities predict where and under what conditions diseases are most likely to emerge.

"If you're surprised by every disease event, you're running around chasing all the wrong things," Karesh said. "If something occurs in an unusual place or under unusual conditions, it leads you to think it was either intentional or accidental," such as a lab error.

Much of the preparation for infectious disease outbreaks will pay off regardless of the cause of the outbreak, Karesh said. "It doesn't matter whether it's intentional or accidental or natural—we need to be equally prepared."

Many of the roles played by federal, state and local emergency management agencies would be similar in any kind of attack or disaster, whether it's a chemical or biological weapon, a bomb or a hurricane. But there are a few government roles that are specific to public health disasters.

One of the main roles is mass prophylaxis, Casagrande said. If there is a biological attack using a bacterial agent, for example, "getting antibiotics out into the population can make or break your response because you can prevent the illness in a large number of people. Otherwise you could end up treating thousands of the critically ill."

The federal government keeps stockpiles of drugs such as antibiotics and vaccines that would be needed to respond to various biological or chemical attacks. State and local governments are in charge of distributing them in case of an emergency. The goal is to be able to distribute antibiotics, for example, to everyone who needs them within 48 hours—an extremely challenging goal, Casagrande said.

Actually distributing the drugs to a panicked population could prove extremely difficult, said Casagrande. Among the questions that must be addressed:

If a Local Government Has Identified Specific Places for Distribution but the Agent Involved Could Cause Contamination, Should Officials Wait to See Where the Contamination Is Before Setting Up the Distribution Sites?

"Either way there's a downside," Casagrande said. Testing first risks overburdening a smaller number of sites and not getting the drugs to everyone in time. But going ahead with the distribution could expose more people as they come to contaminated areas to receive the drugs.

If the Plan Calls for Distributing Drugs Over Multiple Days, Does Everyone Wait in Line? If So, How Will They Be Sheltered and Fed? If Not, Is There a Lottery System for Determining the Order of Distribution? What Is the Most Effective Use of Security Personnel?

In an emergency, law enforcement will have many competing priorities, like keeping order at hospitals and, in the case of an attack, tracking down the perpetrators, in addition to helping secure distribution centers.

State and local governments have their own strategies for handling these issues, said Casagrande, "but some strategies are better than others."

Biological or chemical weapons can be very sophisticated or extremely simple. Some attacks may cause economic harm by targeting livestock or crops (even if the illness is not transmitted to people this way).

For terrorists, Karesh said, "it's not about the outcome—it's about the psychological disruption."

The most sophisticated attacks would come from groups, such as governments, with a lot of money: "You could design and build a very sophisticated device to spread the organism of your choice in some effective way," said Karesh. "If you don't have any money, you could just walk into a cow field where there's foot-and-mouth disease and then come to the United States and walk around with your same muddy boots and introduce foot-and-mouth disease. All you need is a pair of shoes and an airline ticket." A foot-and-mouth disease outbreak, he noted, would devastate US cattle ranchers.

How can government at all levels be more prepared to respond to an outbreak caused by chemical or biological agents? Karesh offers a number of areas for focus and change:

Create Stable Policies and Funding

"We see this roller coaster of investments in the most recent crisis, and three years later there's no more support or funding," Karesh said. "Essential programs shouldn't just come and go. We deserve stable, long-term approaches."

Centralize Leadership

Karesh sees a need for "strategic thinking at the highest levels of government," with one person ultimately in charge rather than spreading responsibility over many departments.

Strengthen communications between human health experts and those focused on animal health and the environment. When someone shows up in an emergency room with anthrax, "the traditional approach is that we need to notify everybody, thinking this may be a terrorist attack," Karesh said. If the human and animal health experts talk to one another, though, health officials may discover that anthrax has been found in sheep and cattle in the area, leading doctors to ask the patient about exposure to those animals. On the other hand, if the agricultural specialists say they haven't seen any anthrax locally in years, that could send the investigation in a different direction.

"It's about preparedness, having your network of people you can trust," Karesh said. This means less time wasted when an emergency occurs. "You don't want to be meeting each other and exchanging business cards during a crisis."

Focus on Patterns

Since authorities can't monitor everything all the time, it makes sense to use data to narrow the focus. For example, some areas of the world have a higher risk of producing diseases than others, and travel patterns make it possible to predict which areas of the United States are most likely to receive people from those areas.

Act on Lists of Pathogens of Highest Concern

Now that the government and other researchers have identified agents to be most concerned about, emergency management and public health officials at all levels should make sure they understand their role.

"Does everybody understand how they appear?" Karesh said. "Do we have medical countermeasures prepared, and do we have the supply chain to make sure those are available fast enough?"

In Britain Biological Agents Research Is Recognized as Beneficial

Julian Turner

In the following viewpoint, Julian Turner argues that the British Government is changing its policy on research and development of biological agents. Turner explains that the basis for the change is the belief that research into chemical and biological agents might lead to beneficial products such as vaccines. Turner is a frequent contributor to the online publication Army Technology.

As you read, consider the following questions:

1. What does the "dual-use dilemma" mean as defined in this viewpoint?
2. According to Turner, what does the Biological and Toxic Weapons Convention do?
3. Why does the UK want to collaborate with biological weapons experts according to the author?

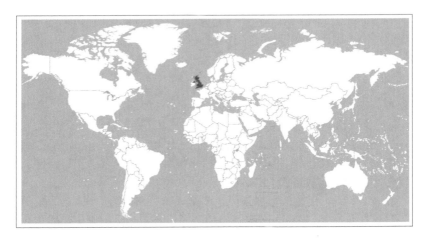

"When you see something that is technically sweet, you go ahead and do it and you argue about what to do about it only after you have had your technical success."
– Robert Oppenheimer, testifying at a US Government security hearing in 1954

The "father of the atomic bomb" was referring to science in general and nuclear weapons in particular, but Oppenheimer neatly articulated what is now known as "the dual-use dilemma," the ethical quandary that arises when the same scientific work can be used to do both good and harm—and it is unclear how to prevent misuse without sacrificing beneficial applications.

For while the decision to use nuclear weapons against the cities of Hiroshima and Nagasaki undoubtedly accelerated the end of the Second World War, it also resulted in the deaths of an estimated 185,000 Japanese, ushering in a Cold War that would endure for a half-century and a global arms race that continues to this day.

The dual-use debate recently resurfaced with the news that scientists in the US and Netherlands are to resume research into the spread of the deadly H5N1 strain of bird flu, a year after the US National Science Advisory Board for Biosecurity (NSABB) caused outrage in scientific circles by censoring key parts of the teams' findings.

The reason for the NSABB's decision? It was concerned that terrorists would use the details to develop a biological weapon.

The Biological Non-Proliferation Programme

The controversy coincides with the publication last week of the UK Government's Biological Non-Proliferation Programme. Managed by the UK Ministry of Defence (MoD) and co-authored by the Foreign Secretary William Hague, it outlines how Britain plans to address potential proliferation risks in the biological sciences, where the dual-use dilemma is most problematic.

It contains evidence that Britain's present and future policy on biological weapons is changing and that the British Government—and by association its international allies—clearly believes that the potential benefits of dual-use research outweigh the inherent risks.

The journalist I.F. Stone once commented that the *Washington Post* was a great newspaper because "you never know on what page you will find a page-one story." In this case, that story is up front.

"Work includes redirection of former weapons scientists and seeks to engage more widely with people whose scientific expertise could be misused for weapons purposes," the report states, before going on to say: "Activities will continue to focus on engagement with biological scientists and provide support for the safe and secure development of 'dual use' biological science."

In other words, the UK Government plans to foster collaboration with former biological weapons experts and support exploration into chemical and biological agents that could potentially be used as weapons of mass destruction.

The report even devotes a paragraph to an explanation of the dual-use dilemma: "A key feature of biological science is that much work with naturally occurring pathogens is potentially 'dual use.'"

This means it can either be used for beneficial purposes—such as development of vaccines to prevent disease—or misused for harmful purposes deliberately to cause disease.

"As a result, efforts to reduce the risks of misuse can at the same time provide benefits such as contributing to improved public, veterinary and plant health in the donor and beneficiary states, for example through better understanding of diseases and their causes, and the development of measures to respond to disease outbreaks."

Time to Get Real: Britain's Future Biological Weapons Policy

So, what are the potential implications for Britain's future biological weapons strategy?

Firstly, the UK Government and its G8 allies have reiterated their belief that chemical, biological, radiological and nuclear (CBRN) weapons continue to represent a clear and present danger to military personnel and civilian populations, as evidenced by worldwide government spending on CBRN defence products and services, which reached a new high of $8.38bn in 2011.

Secondly, the Biological Non-Proliferation Programme is arguably an example of realpolitik. Banning dual-use scientific research such as that being conducted into the H5N1 strain of avian flu—work that could potentially produce a vaccine capable of saving millions of lives during a future pandemic—is politically risky and could alienate the scientific community.

It can also be argued that in a world where the raw materials to make CBRN weapons are shockingly easy to acquire, it makes strategic sense to engage with former weapons scientists, in order to gain vital intelligence about how and where biological weapons are manufactured and stored.

Finally, in the internet age, when information published in a Western scientific journal is instantly accessible around the world to anyone with a laptop, preventing the spread of information in the public domain is unrealistic and cripplingly expensive in terms of resources.

The success of this policy is dependent upon the collective will of Britain's G8 allies, otherwise known as the Global Partnership nations. To this end, the Biological Non-Proliferation Programme supports the goals and principles agreed upon at the 2002 G8 Summit in Kananaskis, Canada, including full implementation of the Biological and Toxin Weapons Convention (BTWC), which prohibits the development, production, acquisition, stockpiling or retention of biological weapons.

The UK Government has also signed agreements with the US Department of State (DoS), the World Health Organisation (WHO) and the World Organisation for Animal Health (OIE), under which it will contribute funding to major projects aimed at strengthening biological safety and security in Afghanistan and Iraq. These include training in bio-safety, modern diagnostics and disease surveillance, as well as technical advice and training for laboratories holding dangerous pathogens.

In addition, the National Counter Proliferation Strategy announced in March 2012 pledges to stop countries such as Iran and North Korea from obtaining WMD or advanced conventional weapons.

Necessary Evil? Mitigating the Threat of CBRN Weapons

In December, the dual-use dilemma returned to the top of the global news agenda when William Hague cited evidence that the Syrian Government, led by President Bashar al-Assad, is preparing to use chemical weapons on its own people.

Syria, which has neither signed the Chemical Weapons Convention (CWC) nor ratified the Biological and Toxin Weapons Convention (BTWC), is believed to possess mustard gas and sarin; the CIA believes it may have tried to develop more toxic and persistent nerve agents, such as VX gas.

A report citing Turkish, Arab and Western intelligence agencies put the nation's stockpile at approximately 1,000 tonnes of chemical weapons, stored in 50 towns and cities.

In the wake of the terrorist attacks on 11 September 2001, some US commentators argued that reports such as those detailing the accidental creation of a vaccine resistant mousepox virus and the synthesis of poliovirus provided a blueprint for bio-weapon development by terrorists and should not have been published.

With the release of the Biological Non-Proliferation Programme, the UK Government has stated its belief that dual-use research can help make the world a safer place rather than a more dangerous one—and that the most effective way of preventing CBRN weapons from falling into the wrong hands is to keep its friends close, but its (former) enemies closer.

Researchers Hope to Develop Treatments to Save Lives After Poisoning

Janice Chambers

In the following viewpoint, Janice Chambers reports on her research and work as a toxicologist. She and her team are working to find drugs that can treat the effects of insecticides and nerve agent weapons. Janice Chambers is the director at the Center for Environmental Health Sciences at Mississippi State University, and professor at the Veterinary College.

As you read, consider the following questions:

1. As defined in the viewpoint, what is the blood-brain barrier?
2. What is the goal of the CounterACT program according to Chambers?
3. What chemical group do nerve agents belong to according to the author?

Terror on a Tokyo subway, 1995; attacks on Syrian civilians, 2013 and 2017; assassinations in an airport in Kuala Lumpur, 2017; attempted assassination in London, 2018. Tremors, foaming at the mouth, seizures, respiratory shutdown, sometimes death.

What do these events have in common? Poisoning via a nerve agent—a chemical warfare substance that disrupts communication between the nervous system and muscles and organs.

A major concern for survivors of nerve agent poisoning is the potential for permanent brain damage caused by seizures. Because the brain cannot easily repair such damage, there is a critical need for an antidote that can enter the brain and reverse the early biochemicial effects before harm occurs. Current antidotes, such as 2-PAM, the only FDA-approved reactivator drug in the US, cannot do this because it is unable to cross the blood-brain barrier, a layer of cells between the blood and the brain which prevents many chemicals, such as some drugs, from moving from the blood into the brain.

I am a toxicologist in the Center for Environmental Health Sciences in the College of Veterinary Medicine at Mississippi State University (MSU) where I initially worked on toxic responses in laboratory animals to organophosphate insecticides, a widely used class of crop protection chemicals. Organophosphate insecticides have a similar mechanism of action to nerve agents, but are much less toxic and are only approved by the US Environmental Protection Agency for uses that are not going to be harmful to humans or the ecosystem.

For the past eight years, my team has been developing antidotes that improve survival rates after nerve agent exposure, and we've shown the potential of our new molecules to enter the brain in tests with animals. If approved, these antidotes would give more confidence to both warfighters and civilians that not only could their lives be saved but also their brain function could be preserved.

From Insecticides to Chemical Warfare

Because pesticides are so important to successful agriculture, my group was initially interested in toxic responses to organophosphate insecticides (OPs). My lab focused on the more biological effects, while my husband, Howard Chambers, synthesized chemicals useful to study the toxic effects of these insecticides.

How Chemical Weapons Became Taboo

The world has witnessed two very different chemical weapons attacks in the last two months: in March, the assassination attempt against Sergei Skripal in the British town of Salisbury, and then the Assad regime's latest chemical strike in Syria. The weapons used in both cases are prohibited under international law, and their use indicates the breaking of a "taboo" which has provoked a swift and forceful response from the international community.

But why is this taboo still so powerful? After all, the Skripal poisoning was an assassination attempt, not a mass casualty attack, and fatalities in chemical attacks make up only a small proportion of the towering death toll in Syria's calamitous eight-year-old civil war. Why does the use of chemical weapons provoke such a profound international reaction—and when did these weapons become "special"?

Along with biological and nuclear weapons, chemical weapons have been labelled weapons of mass destruction (WMD) since 1946. The three types of WMD are perceived as a single distinct category of weapons by virtue of their ability to create lasting and indiscriminate harm. Labelling them as distinctively appalling has proved an effective device to galvanise international action to prevent their future use and proliferation.

Both chemical and biological weapons can be used to target populations beyond the battlefield, thus highlighting their indiscriminate nature. Governments feared that technological innovation could lead to even more deadly methods of warfare. They were prohibited in 1925 by the Geneva Protocol, specifically the "Protocol for the Prohibition of the Use in War of Asphyxiating, Poisonous or Other Gases, and of Bacteriological Methods of Warfare."

In the 1980s, it became clear that the international proscription of chemical weapons had not succeeded. The world was subjected to nightmarish images from the 1980–1988 Iran-Iraq War of people suffering from the effects of mustard gas, sarin and tabun. When Iraq used gas to massacre thousands of civilians at Halabja in 1988, the ensuing horror and moral outrage spurred the creation of the 1992 Convention on the Development, Production, Stockpiling and Use of Chemical Weapons. And once again, the norm that all WMD are different from other weapons was reinforced.

"How Chemical Weapons Became Taboo—and Why They Still Are," by Patricia Shamai, The Conversation, 05/23/2018. https://theconversation. com/how-chemical-weapons-became-taboo-and-why-they-still-are-95738. Licensed under CC BY-ND 4.0 International.

OPs were originally developed as insecticides in Germany prior to World War II. This agricultural effort was co-opted by the Nazis to create the first nerve agents: tabun and sarin. Although these agents were not used during World War II and were banned by the Chemical Weapons Convention of 1997, they have been used occasionally in conflicts such as in the Iran-Iraq war.

However, scientists in some countries have continued to design even more dangerous OP compounds. The Novichok agents, suspected of being used in the attempted poisoning of former Russian double agent Sergei Skripal and his daughter Yulia, for example, are estimated to be between eight and 10 times more potent than VX, one of the most toxic of the traditional nerve agents. These highly toxic chemicals are a danger not only to the military but also to civilians who may be exposed during terrorist attacks, by assassins or rogue governments.

In 2010, the direction of my research changed course when one of my former PhD students, who then worked in the Department of Defense's Defense Threat Reduction Agency (DTRA), returned to MSU for a visit and mentioned that one of the military's most pressing needs in warfighter defense was a brain-penetrating AChE reactivator. During that conversation in a local sandwich shop, Howard pulled out his ever-present mechanical pencil and sketched out an oxime—a molecule that could "grab" the nerve agent and remove it from its target—that he thought would be able to cross the blood-brain barrier. The blood-brain barrier is an almost impenetrable layer of cells that make up the brain capillaries that prevent many foreign chemicals from entering the brain, particularly if they are electrically charged.

The former student was impressed and encouraged us to apply for funding from DTRA for synthesizing and testing a platform of novel oximes, based on the structure on that napkin. The oximes that we have invented in our lab are positively charged, like 2-PAM, but are less water soluble, which may prevent the brain's transporters from exporting them out of the brain once they enter. After initial successes, we are now supported by the

National Institutes of Health's CounterACT program, whose goal is protecting civilians from terrorist attacks or chemical accidents.

Nerve Agent Effects

Nerve agents like sarin, VX and Novichok are organophosphate chemicals, and they wreak havoc by inhibiting a critical enzyme in the nervous system called acetylcholinesterase (AChE). What AChE does for a living, so to speak, is to rapidly degrade acetylcholine (ACh), an important chemical that mediates precise and rapid information flow within the brain and to muscles and glands. When AChE is inhibited, acetylcholine builds up and leads to inappropriate and massive stimulation within the nervous system, resulting in life-threatening symptoms: paralysis of the respiratory muscles, narrowing of the trachea and excessive mucus production throughout the respiratory tract so that air cannot pass through. This causes the foaming at the mouth that we see in news coverage of chemical attacks. Death usually results from respiratory failure. The incredible potency of the nerve agents makes them among the most poisonous synthetic chemicals ever produced.

In survivors, prolonged and repeated seizures caused by high quantities of ACh in the brain can cause permanent brain damage.

The antidote for OP poisoning has traditionally included artificial respiration and injections of the drug atropine, which helps the victim to keep breathing. In the US, medics also use an oxime reactivator—called 2-PAM—which restores AChE activity by removing the nerve agent; and benzodiazepine is used to suppress seizures.

The most effective oxime reactivators have a positive charge. But the blood-brain barrier which exists between brain cells and blood capillaries does a good job of blocking these charged chemicals from infiltrating the brain, either by preventing entry or escorting them out once they enter. Therefore, 2-PAM and other approved oximes do not reach high enough levels in the brain to reverse the deadly grasp of OP nerve agents.

A Promising New Antidote

To protect people from nerve agent poisoning, we need a brain-penetrating molecule to reverse the AChE inhibition. Our lab group and several others worldwide are attempting to create such an antidote that restores AChE activity in the brain following severe OP poisoning.

To date, several of our oxime drugs have been as good as or more effective than 2-PAM for increasing 24-hour survival for animals exposed to lethal doses of OPs, using highly relevant mimics of two nerve agents sarin and VX, as well as an insecticidal chemical in a laboratory animal model.

We have convincing evidence that our oximes can get through the blood-brain barrier and enter the brain after OP exposure, and that our laboratory animals show more normal activity of AChE with our novel oximes but not with 2-PAM. Our animals also recovered more quickly from seizure-like behavior with our oxime antidote compared to 2-PAM. Our lead oxime seems likely to remain in the brain, and it has prevented some damage to brain structures, while 2-PAM did not—a finding we describe in an upcoming publication.

This oxime platform has been patented by MSU and licensed by Defender Pharmaceuticals. Sadly, my long-term collaborator, Howard, passed away in December 2016; my team continues to pursue the research needed to develop his novel oximes into antidotes.

What value could these novel oximes bring to the arsenal of chemical weapon antidotes? Either alone, or in combination with 2-PAM, they could contribute to survival and, uniquely, they could reduce or prevent the brain damage caused by the prolonged seizures induced by OPs.

In other words, with our novel antidotes we could save lives and save brains.

Periodical and Internet Sources Bibliography

The following articles have been selected to supplement the diverse views presented in this chapter.

Larry Abramson, "Why Chemical Weapons Have Been a Red Line Since World War I," NPR, May 1, 2013. https://www.npr.org/2013/05/01/180348908/why-chemical-weapons-have-been-a-red-line-since-world-war-i.

Ken Chambelain, "X-Ray Bombs: When Conventional Bombs Just Won't Do," *Tech Watch*, July 2, 2018. https://www.defensenews.com/industry/techwatch/2018/07/02/x-ray-bombs-when-conventional-explosives-just-wont-do/.

Wanglai Gao, "Unearthing Poison: Disposal of Abandoned Chemical Weapons in China," *Bulletin of the Atomic Scientists*, November 2, 2017. https://thebulletin.org/2017/11/unearthing-poison-disposal-of-abandoned-chemical-weapons-in-china/.

Andrew Hessel, "Hacking the President's DNA," *The Atlantic*, November 2012. https://www.theatlantic.com/magazine/archive/2012/11/hacking-the-presidents-dna/309147/.

Jennifer S. Love, MD, "A Review of Chemical Warfare Agents and Treatment Options," *Journal of Emergency Medical Services*, September 1, 2017. https://www.jems.com/articles/print/volume-42/issue-9/features/a-review-of-chemical-warfare-agents-and-treatment-options.html.

William Schabas, "Why Are Chemical Weapons Worse Than Other Weapons of Mass Destruction?" *The Guardian*, April 25, 2018. https://www.theguardian.com/commentisfree/2018/apr/25/chemical-weapons-mass-destruction-syria-nuclear.

Tonia Twichell, "The Risk is Only Going to Grow," CU School of Medicine, December 2017. http://www.ucdenver.edu/academics/colleges/medicalschool/administration/alumni/CUMedToday/profiles/Pages/Antidote-for-Chemical-Weapons.aspx.

CHAPTER 3

Why Do Terrorists Use Chemical and Biological Weapons?

Countries May Be Circumventing the Verification Regime of the Biological Weapons Convention

Mike Nartker

In the following viewpoint, intended to provide historical perspective, Mike Nartker reports that according to a 2005 CIA prediction, a terrorist group is likely to use biological weapons in an attack by 2020. Nartker writes that the US will continue to be a target for terrorists, and that Western Europe and the Middle East might too. Some countries may be developing chemical and biological weapons under the cover of legitimate organizations, he predicted, and threats may become more difficult to detect. Mike Nartker writes for the NIT, the Nuclear Threat Initiative.

As you read, consider the following questions:

1. According to Nartker's 2005 perspective, how would terrorist groups change by 2020? How have the CIA's predictions proved correct or incorrect?
2. As reported by the viewpoint, how might terrorists obtain a nuclear weapon?
3. What group may be dealing in weapons of mass destruction, as predicted by the viewpoint?

"Terrorists Likely to Conduct Biological Attack by 2020, U.S. Intelligence Report Warns," by Mike Nartker, Nuclear Threat Initiative, January 14, 2005. Reprinted by permission.

A terrorist group is "likely" to conduct an attack using biological weapons by 2020, according to a report released yesterday by a CIA think-tank.

Over the next 15 years, successes in the global war on terrorism and advances in information technology are likely to result in an increasingly "decentralized" terrorist threat, consisting of an "eclectic array of groups, cells and individuals," says the report, prepared by the National Intelligence Council. While influenced by al-Qaeda, such smaller groups are expected to overshadow the terrorist organization by 2020 and could recruit new members through the war in Iraq and other possible conflicts, the report says.

Acts of bioterrorism would be "particularly suited" to these smaller and better-informed terrorist groups, the report says.

"Indeed, the bioterrorist's laboratory could well be the size of a household kitchen, and the weapon built there could be smaller than a toaster. Terrorist use of biological agents is therefore likely, and the range of options will grow," it says.

The report also warns that while it is "less likely" terrorists would obtain a nuclear weapon; they are expected to continue to attempt to do so over the next 15 years through theft or purchase, "particularly in Russia or Pakistan." The likelihood that a terrorist attack involving a nuclear weapon occurs before 2020 "cannot be ruled out," it adds.

Even so, the report says that most terrorist attacks in the future are expected to continue to involve conventional weapons, though with "new twists to keep counterterrorist planners off balance." Among such possible new strategies are the use of simultaneous attacks in widely separated areas, the use of advanced explosives and unmanned aerial vehicles (UAVs) and possible cyber attacks against computer systems and information networks.

The United States and its interests will continue to be "prime terrorist targets," but increasingly attacks may also focus on Western Europe and other Middle East countries, the report says.

The report is the third to be released by the National Intelligence Council, with previous reports covering periods through 2010 and 2015. It is based on discussions held with more than 1,000 independent experts over the past year, according to reports.

"Mindful that there are many possible 'futures,' our report offers a range of possibilities and potential discontinuities, as a way of opening our minds to developments we might otherwise miss," council chairman Robert Hutchings said in an introductory letter.

Along with terrorists seeking weapons of mass destruction, the report warns that a number of countries will continue to seek, and in some cases "enhance," their own such armaments. Nuclear weapons states are expected over the next 15 years to improve the survivability of their forces, to improve their nuclear delivery systems and to develop the capability to penetrate missile defense systems, the report says.

In an apparent reference to the suspected nuclear weapons programs of Iran and North Korea, the report also says that other non-nuclear countries, especially in the Middle East and Northeastern Asia, may choose to develop atomic weapons "as it becomes clear that their neighbors and regional rivals are already doing so." Those efforts may be accelerated through proliferators like the former associates of Pakistani nuclear scientist Abdul Qadeer Khan, who has confessed to transferring nuclear weapons technology to Iran, Libya and North Korea.

The concern that the nuclear efforts of Iran and North Korea may prompt others to follow suit has been "widely held" among proliferation experts for years, said Daryl Kimball, executive director of the Arms Control Association.

"It doesn't take a national intelligence expert to figure that out," he said today.

Countries are expected to continue to hide biological and chemical weapons production capabilities through incorporation into legitimate commercial infrastructures and are expected to be less reliant on foreign suppliers, the report says. It also warns of the development of advanced biological weapons agents and the possible development of chemical agents intended to circumvent the verification regime of the Chemical Weapons Convention.

Kimball said that "not too much is being done" to address the advancing biological weapons threat. As countermeasures, he recommended increasing efforts to have private industry self-regulate biological research, to have government oversight of some research and the development of a verification regime for the Biological Weapons Convention. "Nothing of substance" is being done now on such measures, Kimball said.

Countries are also expected to continue development of improved ballistic and cruise missiles, as well as unmanned aerial vehicles, over the next 15 years, according to the report. By 2010, several countries of concerns will probably acquire land-attack cruise missiles and North Korea and Iran are almost certain to have developed ICBM capabilities, it says. In [addition], several other countries are likely by 2010 to have developed space launch vehicles, which can be used to aid ICBM development, the report adds.

There is also increasing concern that organized crime groups may increasingly deal in weapons of mass destruction over the next 15 years if countries "lose control of their inventories," the report says.

The Ebola Virus Probably Won't Make an Effective Weapon, but Instilling Fear Might Be Enough

Jamie Doward

In the following viewpoint, Jamie Doward reports on a research unit that is assessing the potential use of the Ebola virus as an agent of bioterrorism. Doward includes the opionions of various experts when she argues that the Ebola virus doesn't make a viable choice as a biological agent for a variety of reasons. However, instilling fear of even the threat of an attack is an effective tactic of terrorists. Jamie Doward is a frequent contributor to The Guardian.

As you read, consider the following questions:

1. According to this viewpoint, what virus may be weaponized by terrorists?
2. At the time of this viewpoint, what three countries were most affected by Ebola?
3. How many people are infected by the average Ebola carrier, as reported by this viewpoint?

Scientists at the top-secret military research unit at Porton Down, Wiltshire, have been assessing the potential use of Ebola as a bioterrorism weapon, according to confidential documents.

A three-page memo, marked "UK secret UK eyes only," reveals that the unit, where chemical, radiological and biological threats are analysed, was tasked with evaluating whether terrorist organisations such as al-Qaeda and Islamic State (ISIS) could use the deadly virus to attack western targets.

The heavily redacted document, which has been released under the Freedom of Information Act, reveals that the unit was asked last October to provide "guidance on the feasibility and potential impact of a non-state actor exploiting the Ebola outbreak in west Africa for bioterrorism."

It goes on to explain that non-state actor threat assessments are "provided by the joint terrorism analysis centre," while threats to "UK deployed forces are provided by defence intelligence." The memo outlines three possible scenarios under which terrorists might seek to exploit the Ebola outbreak, which so far has killed more than 9,000 people in the three most affected countries, Guinea, Sierra Leone and Liberia.

The first scenario outlined is completely redacted, illustrating the acute sensitivity about the issue. The second scenario is heavily blacked out but, according to the memo, "would be both logistically and technically challenging for a non-state group to undertake." It observes: "Clearly there are practical issues involved with such a scenario that of themselves are often not insurmountable but taken together add enormously to the complexity of successfully undertaking this attack."

A third, also heavily redacted, scenario "constitutes the most technically challenging of the scenarios considered here."

Concerns that terrorist groups might look to "weaponise" Ebola have been raised by several thinktanks and politicians. Last year Francisco Martinez, Spain's state secretary for security, claimed that ISIS fighters were planning to carry out "lone wolf" attacks using biological weapons. Martinez said that his belief was informed by listening in to conversations uncovered in secret chatrooms used by terrorist cells. The claim has since been played down by others.

Jeh Johnson, the US Department of Homeland Security secretary, said last October that "we've seen no specific credible intelligence that ISIS is attempting to use any sort of disease or virus to attack our homeland."

Dr. Filippa Lentzos, a senior research fellow at King's College London and an expert on bioterrorism, said terrorists looking to use the virus as a weapon would encounter problems. "It doesn't spread quickly at all," she said. "Terrorists are usually after a bang and Ebola isn't going to give you that."

On average, a person infected with Ebola will infect two more people. In a developed country such as the UK transmission would be even more limited.

"People with Ebola are infectious only when they show symptoms," Lentzos said. "Could terrorists go to west Africa, get infected, then come back and sit on the tube? Sure, but they're not likely to be functional for very long. They're going to be very sick and you'll see that. So they would have only a very small window in which to operate. And in a country with a developed public health system like the UK, there would be plenty of chances to clamp down on an outbreak."

Other biological weapons would potentially be more attractive to terrorists, experts suggested. Unlike Ebola, which requires the transmission of body fluids, anthrax spores can be dried and milled down to form tiny particles that can be inhaled.

However, even the suggestion that Ebola could be weaponised made it a potentially powerful weapon for terrorists, Lentzos suggested. "If your aim is not to kill a lot of people, or even make them ill, but instead to frighten them and cause a huge level of societal disruption, then bioterrorism would do that. It elicits exceptionally high levels of fear, disgust and abhorrence."

The use of pathogens as a weapon has been tried before. Following the attacks in New York and Washington in 2001, five people died in the US after opening letters laced with anthrax. In the 1980s, a cult in Oregon spread salmonella on salad bars in restaurants in an attempt to keep voters from the polls so its preferred candidates would win.

"The risk of small-scale bioterrorism attacks is possible and very likely," Lentzos said.

Porton Down is known to have experimented with Ebola but a specific request for the laboratory to analyse the virus's potential use by "non-state agents" highlights the growing concern that terrorists are becoming increasingly inventive in their choice of weapons.

One scenario could see terrorists combining genes from different pathogens to synthetically create super pathogens that could spread disease far more effectively than Ebola. But Lentzos suggested this was unlikely. "It's pretty damn hard to make dangerous pathogens from scratch in the lab. Experts have a really hard time doing that. At this point I'm not sure that's what we need to worry about."

Lentzos said that focusing on the terrorist threat posed by Ebola risked losing sight of the bigger picture. "To beat Ebola we have to worry less about terrorism and more about public health. Disease knows no borders."

Chemical and Biological Terrorism Can Cause More Damage Than Conventional Terrorism

Aimee Amiga and Ruth Schuster

In the following viewpoint, Aimee Amiga and Ruth Schuster maintain that ISIS is most likely working up to launching a bioterrorist attack. The authors contend that ISIS is using chemical and biological agents that they have found in areas they have overtaken, and might have the know how to produce or weaponize these things. Aimee Amiga is a reporter and editor and Ruth Schuster is senior editor at Haaretz.com the online edition of Haaretz Daily Newspaper *in Israel.*

As you read, consider the following questions:

1. According to the authors, what chemical did ISIS use against the Kurds?
2. What might deter ISIS from using biological weapons, as stated in the viewpoint?
3. How might the West frustrate terrorist efforts as outlined by the authors?

C ould Islamic State carry out chemical or biological terrorism in Europe? Yes, and it might, warns a briefing to the European Parliament published this week, saying that the radical Islamic

"EU Report: ISIS Could Commit Chemical or Biological Terror Attack in West," by Aimee Amiga and Ruth Schuster, Haaretz Daily Newspaper Ltd, December 13, 2015. Reprinted by permission.

group has money; scientists—some of foreign origin—on the payroll; found an abundance of deadly toxins stockpiled by the tyrants of Syria, Iraq and Libya; and could make more of its own quite easily.

"European citizens are not seriously contemplating the possibility that extremist groups might use chemical, biological, radiological or nuclear materials during attacks in Europe," writes analyst Beatriz Immenkamp in the briefing. They should.

It wouldn't be a big leap. ISIS has used mustard and chlorine gases in Iraq and Syria. And a laptop belonging to a Tunisian physicist who joined ISIS was found to contain a paper on weaponizing bubonic plague bacteria obtained from animals. The intent is there: the governments of Belgium and France are already working on contingency plans.

Moreover, it would be fairly simple for ISIS sympathizers to obtain the materials for chemical and biological attacks in Europe itself, the report says. The continent is brimming with them and security is inadequate.

Israeli experts add that the group could make deadly chemicals of its own, and could be already developing the capacity to weaponize them.

DIY Mass War

At least some chemical weapons, whether gaseous, liquid or solid, are fairly trivial to make. To attack the Kurds, for example, says the EU report, it appears that ISIS simply repurposed fertilizer.

Making—or obtaining—the chemical is the first stage. The second is weaponizing it. Can ISIS make its own chemical weapons?

ISIS may have manufactured crude shells containing toxic chemicals, the EU report says. "[Weaponization] can be done crudely by putting the substance into shells and firing those shells," says Dany Shoham, a specialist in unconventional weapons from the Begin Sadat Center of Strategic Studies at Bar Ilan University.

Indeed, ISIS' use of chemical weapons has been crude so far, but the group could become more sophisticated in their weaponization in the future, he suggests.

Alternatively, ISIS could capture already weaponized chemicals. It is probable that ISIS has deployed both weapons it made itself and weapons it captured, says Shoham.

As for resources: In June 2014, ISIS seized control of Muthanna, Iraq, once the Saddam Hussein regime's primary chemical-weapons production facility. American troops were supposed to have destroyed weapons there after the 2003 invasion of Iraq, but officials admitted when ISIS conquered the city that a stockpile of weapons still existed. They claimed the remaining chemical weapons had no military value. The following month, ISIS launched its first chemical attack on the Kurds in Kobani, Syria, using mustard gas, an agent that is known to have been made at Muthanna.

ISIS may also have access to weapons containing sarin nerve gas that remained in Syria, the EU report notes, as well as mustard agents and nerve agent rockets from Iraq, and chemical materials leftover from Libya programs.

It is unclear how effective these agents would be after years of storage, qualifies Ely Karmon, a specialist in terrorism and chemical, biological, radiological and nuclear weapons at the International Institute for Counter-Terrorism at the Interdisciplinary Center Herzliya. But they might still be usable.

In addition, ISIS has a lot of scientific talent on board, including some inherited from the Hussein regime, says Karmon. For instance, until his death in a coalition strike in January, ISIS had Hussein's chemical warfare expert Salih Jasim Muhammed Falah al-Sabawi, aka Abu Malik, on the payroll. The United States said Abu Malik provided ISIS with "expertise to pursue a chemical weapons capability."

Possessing chemical weapons does not necessarily mean the group can use them beyond the borders of Syria and Iraq. "Transferring chemical weapons to Europe would be difficult," says

Keeping a Watchful Eye

Rapid advances in gene editing and so-called "DIY biological laboratories" which could be used by extremists, threaten to derail efforts to prevent biological weapons from being used against civilians, the world's only international forum on the issue has heard.

At meetings taking place at the United Nations in Geneva which ended on Thursday, representatives from more than 100 Member States which have signed up to the Biological Weapons Convention (BWC)—together with civilian experts and academics—also discussed how they could ensure that science is used to positive ends, in line with the disarmament blueprint set out by UN Secretary-General António Guterres.

Although the potential impact of a biological weapons attack could be huge, the likelihood is not currently believed to be high. The last attack dates back to 2001, when letters containing toxic anthrax spores, killed five people in the US, just days after al-Qaeda terrorists perpetrated the 9/11 attacks on New York and Washington.

In a bid to stay on top of the latest biological developments and threats, the BWC's 181 Member States hold a series of meetings with experts every year, traditionally in the summer. The reports that are discussed during these sessions are then [formally] appraised in December.

At the eight-day session [that] just ended, science and technology issues were debated for two days—a measure of their importance.

Among the developments discussed was the groundbreaking gene-editing technique CRISPR. It can be applied—in theory—to any organism. Outside the Geneva body, CRISPR's use has raised ethical questions, Mr. Feakes said, but among Member States, security ramifications dominated discussions.

"Potentially, it could be used to develop more effective biological weapons," he said, noting that the meetings addressed the growing trend of "DIY biological labs." However, the meetings also focused on the promotion of "responsible science" so that "scientists are part of the solution, not the problem."

"There are no States that say they need biological weapons," Mr. Feakes says. "That norm needs to be maintained and properly managed. You can't ban CRISPR or gene editing, because they can do so much good, like finding cures for diseases or combating climate change. But we still need to manage these techniques and technologies to ensure they are used responsibly."

"Terrorists Potentially Target Millions in Makeshift Biological Weapons 'Laboratories,'"
Modern Diplomacy, *August 18, 2018. Reprinted by permission.*

Karmon. Weaponizing chemicals within the borders of Europe would also be difficult, adds Shoham, given the likelihood of being detected by security agencies.

However, Shoham and Karmon agree that ISIS could use toxic chemicals in Europe, relatively easily, in an unweaponized form—the impact of such an attack could be devastating, notes Shoham.

Alternatively, ISIS could attack a chemical facility with conventional weapons, similar to Yassin Salhi's failed attempt to strike the Air Products chemical factory near Lyon, France, notes Karmon.

Weaponizing Germs

Biological weapons—germs—are a different story. The science of bio-weaponry has come far since the millennia of yore, when besiegers might toss a disease-riddled corpse over the town walls to terrify and infect the people inside. Today's nightmare scenarios include, for example, weaponized ebola virus that can infect through the air, rather than requiring physical proximity to infected mucous membranes, or anthrax engineered to be even deadlier than the original bacterium.

How easy is it for ISIS to procure or make biological weapons? And if they had them, would they be likely they use them?

Obtaining the bugs at the base of biological weapons wouldn't be a big problem, surmises Shoham. Suitable pathogens are readily available at academic laboratories, vaccine factories and pharmaceutical companies, all of which are civilian facilities. Even if few such institutions still exist in the ISIS territories, the group might try to get bacteria from sympathizers in Europe or the United States, Shoham says.

But for all that telltale laptop of the Tunisian physicist, ISIS would have difficulty weaponizing them, Shoham thinks—yet adds that biological terrorism can also be carried out without weaponization. For example, by releasing a pathogen into a water system.

So ISIS could get the bugs and might be able to weaponize them, or could use them as is. But would the group resort to bio-war?

Working with biological agents is very risky for the handler, Shoham says, but adds: "I don't think this factor would constitute a bottleneck for a radical organization like ISIS."

The obstacle most likely to deter ISIS from deploying biological weapons isn't the risk of some lab technician falling ill. It's their inability to control its spread, says Karmon.

Unlike chemical and radiological weapons, one cannot target a defined set of victims with biological agents because they are contagious, he explains. Anybody using a bio-weapon runs the risk of infecting their own population. That in itself is a powerful deterrent.

Whether it would be enough to deter ISIS from using bioweapons in Europe, given the ability of bacteria to travel on planes, is anybody's guess.

Impact: The Cost of War

Chemical and biological terrorism would probably cause significantly more damage than conventional terrorism, Shoham and Karmon agree.

Even in a best-case scenario, for instance that an infectious agent is detected in the water system before anyone drinks or bathes in it, just cleaning the contaminant from the water system would be very difficult, Shoham says. The EU report notes that in anticipation of this very sort of thing, Paris has stepped up security at its water facilities.

What can the West do to frustrate this threat?

It could try to limit ISIS' access to certain civilian and military installations in Syria and Iraq, says Shoham. Yet, doing this without ground forces may prove difficult.

Might the threat of a massive counter-attack by the West serve as a significant deterrent? Probably not, says Shoham.

Europe can screen travelers entering the continent, says Shoham, although this is unlikely to serve as a rigorous enough preventative measure. The EU report itself suggests monitoring returning fighters and radicals in the European Union, especially any known to have "CBRN [(chemical, biological, radiological and nuclear weapons)] knowledge."

Aside from that, the report suggests that European nations improve preparedness, for instance by equipping rescue forces with antidotes. Europe can also increase security at key installations, which Paris, for one, is already doing. And, in addition, European countries can start preparing and drilling their populations.

During the first Gulf War, the Israeli government began handing out gas masks to the general population. They aren't effective against all forms of chemical attack, let alone biological. A full-body suit is better. But gas masks, used properly, are a good start.

Bioterrorism Is Difficult to Control

Tim Newman

In the following viewpoint, Tim Newman analyzes the answer to his own question of whether society should be worried about a bioterrorist attack. He provides a short history on the use of biological agents through time, and then gives a run down on modern concerns, a list of possible contaminants, and new technology that might prove risky. Tim Newman is the news editor at MNT, Medical News Today, the popular online health information site.

As you read, consider the following questions:

1. What type of agents are used in "germ warfare" according to Newman?
2. As reported in this viewpoint, what agent would most likely be developed for biological weapons use?
3. According to the author, what technology might be a cause for concern?

Sometimes known as "germ warfare," biological weapons involve the use of toxins or infectious agents that are biological in origin. This can include bacteria, viruses, or fungi.

These agents are used to incapacitate or kill humans, animals, or plants as part of a war effort.

In effect, biological warfare is using non-human life to disrupt—or end—human life. Because living organisms can be unpredictable and incredibly resilient, biological weapons are difficult to control, potentially devastating on a global scale, and prohibited globally under numerous treaties.

Of course, treaties and international laws are one thing—and humanity's ability to find innovative ways of killing each other is another.

Biological Warfare: The Early Days

The history of biological warfare is a long one, which makes sense; its deployment can be a lo-fi affair, so there is no need for electrical components, nuclear fusion, or rocket grade titanium, for instance.

An early example takes us back more than 2 and a half millennia: Assyrians infected their enemy's wells with a rye ergot fungus, which contains chemicals related to LSD. Consuming the tainted water produced a confused mental state, hallucinations, and, in some cases, death.

In the 1300s, Tartar (Mongol) warriors besieged the Crimean city of Kaffa. During the siege, many Tartars died at the hands of plague, and their lifeless, infected bodies were hurled over the city walls.

Some researchers believe that this tactic may have been responsible for the spread of Black Death plague into Europe. If so, this early use of biological warfare caused the eventual deaths of around 25 million Europeans.

This is a prime example of biological warfare's potential scope, unpredictability, and terrifying simplicity.

Moving forward to 1763, the British Army attmped to use smallpox as a weapon against Native Americans at the Siege of Fort Pitt. In an attempt to spread the disease to the locals, the Brits presented blankets from a smallpox hospital as gifts.

Although we now know that this would be a relatively ineffective way to transmit smallpox, the intent was there.

During World War II, many of the parties involved looked into biological warfare with great interest. The Allies built facilities capable of mass producing anthrax spores, brucellosis, and botulism toxins. Thankfully, the war ended before they were used.

It was the Japanese who made the most use of biological weapons during World War II, as among other terrifyingly indiscriminate attacks, the Japanese Army Air Force dropped ceramic bombs full of fleas carrying the bubonic plague on Ningbo, China.

The following quote comes from a paper on the history of biological warfare.

> "[T]he Japanese army poisoned more than 1,000 water wells in Chinese villages to study cholera and typhus outbreaks ... Some of the epidemics they caused persisted for years and continued to kill more than 30,000 people in 1947, long after the Japanese had surrendered."
>
> —Dr. Friedrich Frischknecht, professor of integrative parasitology, Heidelberg University, Germany

Bioterrorism: Modern Concerns

The Centers for Disease Control and Prevention (CDC) define bioterrorism as "the intentional release of viruses, bacteria, or other germs that can sicken or kill people, livestock, or crops."

This can be achieved in a number of ways, such as: via aerosol sprays; in explosive devices; via food or water; or absorbed or injected into skin.

Because some pathogens are less robust than others, the type of pathogen used will define how it can be deployed.

Utilizing such weapons holds a certain appeal to terrorists; they have the potential to cause great harm, of course, but they are also fairly cheap to produce when compared with missiles or other more hi-tech equipment.

Also, they can be "detonated," and, due to the long time that it takes for them to spread and take effect, there is plenty of time for the perpetrator to escape undetected.

Biological weapons can be difficult to control or predict in a battlefield situation, since there is a substantial risk that troops on both sides will be affected. However, if a terrorist is interested in attacking a distant target as a lone operant, bioterrorism carries much less risk to the person.

Anthrax

Experts believe that today, the most likely organism to be used in a bioterrorism attack would be *Bacillus anthracis*, the bacteria that causes anthrax.

It is widely found in nature, easily produced in the laboratory, and survives for a long time in the environment. Also, it is versatile and can be released in powders, sprays, water, or food.

Anthrax has been used before. In 2001, anthrax spores were sent through the United States postal system. In all, 22 people contracted anthrax—five of whom died. And, the guilty party was never caught.

Smallpox

Another potential agent of bioterrorism is smallpox, which, unlike anthrax, can spread from person to person. Smallpox is no longer a disease of concern in the natural world—because concerted vaccination efforts stamped it out—and the last naturally spread case occurred in 1977.

However, if someone were to gain access to the smallpox virus (it is still kept in two laboratories—one in the US and one in Russia), it could be an effective weapon, spreading quickly and easily between people.

Plague

We have already mentioned the Tartars' use of the plague, *Yersinia pestis*, hundreds of years ago, but some believe that it could be used in the modern world, too. *Y. pestis* is passed to humans through the bite of a flea that has fed on infected rodents.

Once a human is infected, the resulting disease can either develop into bubonic plague, which is difficult to transmit among humans and fairly easy to treat with antibiotics, or—if the infection spreads to the lungs—it becomes pneumonic plague, which develops rapidly and does not respond well to antibiotics.

A paper written on the plague and its potential for use in biological terrorism says:

"Given the presence and availability of plague around the world, the capacity for mass production and aerosol dissemination, the high fatality rate of pneumonic plague, and the potential for rapid secondary spread, the potential use of plague as a biological weapon is of great concern."

—Dr. Stefan Riedel, Department of Pathology, Baylor University Medical Center, Dallas, TX

Cholera

As a potentially severe and sometimes deadly gastrointestinal disease, cholera has the potential to be used in bioterrorism. It does not spread easily from person to person, so for it to be effective, it would need to be liberally added to a major water source.

In the past, the bacteria responsible for cholera, *Vibrio cholerae*, has been weaponized by the US, Japan, South Africa, and Iraq, among others.

Tularemia

Some consider tularemia, an infection caused by the *Francisella tularensis* bacterium, as a potential bioweapon. It causes fever, ulcerations, swelling of lymph glands, and, sometimes, pneumonia.

The bacterium can cause infection by entering through breaks in the skin or by being breathed into the lungs. It is particularly infectious, and only a very small number of organisms (as few as 10) need to enter the body to set off a serious bout of tularemia.

Studied by the Japanese during World War II and stockpiled by the US in the 1960s, *F. tularensis* is hardy, capable of withstanding low temperatures in water, hay, decaying carcasses, and moist soil for many weeks.

According to the Johns Hopkins Center for Public Health Preparedness, "Aerosol dissemination of *F. tularensis* in a populated area would be expected to result in the abrupt onset of large numbers of cases of acute, non-specific, febrile illness beginning 3 to 5 days later … with pleuropneumonitis developing in a significant proportion of cases."

"Without antibiotic treatment, the clinical course could progress to respiratory failure, shock, and death."

Those pathogens are an abbreviated selection, of course. Others considered to have potential as biological weapons include brucellosis, Q fever, monkeypox, arboviral encephalitides, viral hemorrhagic fevers, and staphylococcal enterotoxin B.

A Worrying Future?

Although biological weapons are as old as the hills (if not older), modern technology brings new worries. Some experts are concerned about recent advances in gene editing technology.

When utilized for good, the latest tools can work wonders. However—as with most cutting-edge technology—there is always the potential for misuse.

A gene editing technology called CRISPR has set off alarm bells in the defense community; the technology allows researchers to edit genomes, thereby easily modifying DNA sequences to alter gene function.

In the right hands, this tool has the potential to correct genetic defects and treat disease. In the wrong hands, however, it has the potential for evil.

CRISPR technology is becoming cheaper to run and therefore more accessible to individuals bent on bioterrorism.

A report titled *Worldwide Threat Assessment of the US Intelligence Community*, written by James Clapper, the director of National Intelligence, was published in February 2016. In it, gene editing features in a list of weapons of mass destruction and proliferation.

"Given the broad distribution, low cost, and accelerated pace of development of this dual-use technology," he explains, "its deliberate or unintentional misuse might lead to far-reaching economic and national security implications."

"Advances in genome editing in 2015," he continues, "have compelled groups of high-profile US and European biologists to question unregulated editing of the human germline (cells that are relevant for reproduction), which might create inheritable genetic changes."

With future generations of CRISPR-like technology and an advanced knowledge of genetics, there would be no theoretical end to the misery that could be caused. There's potential to create drug-resistant strains of diseases, for instance, or pesticide-protected bugs, capable of wiping out a country's staple crop.

For now, however, other methods of bioterrorism are much easier and closer to hand, so this is likely to be of little concern for the foreseeable future.

In fact, to lighten the mood at the end of a somewhat heavy article, just remember that anyone who lives in the US today is much more likely to be killed in an animal attack than a terrorist attack—biological or otherwise.

Easy Availability of Materials Increases the Threat of Chemical and Biological Warfare

Nuclear Threat Initiative

In the following viewpoint, the Nuclear Threat Initiative (NTI) analyzes the threat of bioterrorism from a WMD attack. NTI maintains that the United States and its allies are a target for terrorism by a number of state sponsored groups, perhaps most notably al-Qaeda. The author details nuclear, radiological, and biological weapons. Nuclear Threat Initiative is a nonprofit organization that works to prevent catastrophic attacks from weapons of mass destruction. NTI maintains an online news site, nti.org, which covers nuclear, radiological, and biological threat information.

As you read, consider the following questions:

1. What is a radiological weapon as defined by NTI?
2. According to the viewpoint, how are Russia and the US working together?
3. Which four countries are state sponsors of terrorism according to the viewpoint?

The possibility that a terrorist organization might launch a WMD attack remains one of the "gravest threats" to the

"WMD Terrorism Remains Grave Threat, U.S. Says," Nuclear Threat Initiative, August 6, 2010. Reprinted by permission.

security of the United States and its allies, the US State Department said yesterday in its annual terrorism report.

The *Country Reports on Terrorism 2009* addressed the threat of terrorism involving chemical, biological, radiological and nuclear weapons and Washington's response to those dangers.

The State Department noted that al-Qaeda and other extremist groups have expressed interest in acquiring nuclear weapons.

"The diffusion of scientific and technical information regarding the assembly of nuclear weapons, some of which is now available on the Internet, has increased the risk that a terrorist organization in possession of sufficient fissile material could develop its own crude nuclear weapon," the report says. "The complete production of a nuclear weapon strongly depends on the terrorist group's access to special nuclear materials as well as engineering and scientific expertise."

Due to the proliferation efforts of "irresponsible countries" like North Korea, "the number of potential sources of an unsecured nuclear weapon or materials is challenging worldwide efforts to control and account for nuclear material," according to the State Department. Extremists could also look to underground smuggling networks and international criminal organizations for aid in acquiring or developing nuclear devices, the report says.

While the terrorist detonation of a radiological "dirty bomb" would not be as calamitous as a terrorist nuclear attack, the prevalence of radioactive substances "in nearly every country" means it is much easier to acquire the materials to construct such a weapon, the report says.

"Most radioactive materials lack sufficient strength to present a significant public health risk once dispersed, while the materials posing the greatest hazard would require terrorists to have the expertise to handle them without exposure to incapacitating doses of radiation or detection during transit across international borders," the report says.

However, detonation of a radiological weapon—which would use conventional explosives to disperse radioactive material—could cause a significant amount of panic and financial "disruption," the State Department said.

The report notes the potential for a bioterrorism strike, as "the materials required to produce a biological weapon are available in laboratories worldwide, and many threat agents could be isolated from nature." Al-Qaeda is believed to have pressed harder than other terrorist groups to obtain or produce biological weapons, according to the report, which cites the US discovery of an unfinished laboratory in Afghanistan.

"If properly produced and released, biological agents can kill on a massive scale and, if terrorists use a pathogen that can be transmitted from person to person, the disease could quickly spread through commercial air travel across oceans and continents before authorities realize their nations have been attacked," the report says.

The State Department noted efforts by extremists to acquire and deploy readily available toxic chemicals: "The growth and sophistication of the worldwide chemical industry, including the development of complex synthetic and dual-use materials, may make the task of preventing and protecting against this [chemical weapons] threat more difficult."

In its efforts to combat the threat of a WMD terror attack, the United States has implemented multiple initiatives which include the Global Initiative to Combat Nuclear Terrorism. The initiative is jointly led by Russia and the United States and encompasses 77 members who have given their approval to several central nuclear security principles. Since its inception, the program has carried out 34 multinational operations and held five high-level forums.

The United States has a number of priorities in the effort against WMD terrorism, the report says. These include identifying extremists' "intentions, capabilities and plans" to produce or obtain unconventional weapons and the likelihood of that occurring; preventing terrorists from acquiring the materials, know-how or other means of carrying out such an attack, "with a particular focus on weapons-usable fissile materials, dangerous pathogens and poisonous chemicals"; and deterring would-be attackers and their allies from considering or actually carrying out a strike.

Among the programs used to reduce the WMD terror threat, the report says, are the Proliferation Security Initiative, which is intended to interdict smuggling of WMD materials; the Global Threat Reduction Initiative to secure or eliminate vulnerable nuclear and radioactive materials; and the Global Initiative to Combat Nuclear Terrorism, "a cross-cutting strategic framework of 77 partners and four observers who are determined to strengthen individual and global capacity to prevent, detect, and respond to a nuclear terrorist event" (US State Department report, August 5, 2010).

The report says that last year the al-Qaeda "core in Pakistan remained the foremost security threat to the US homeland," according to a State Department release.

Intelligence agencies found that al-Qaeda entities, notably al-Qaeda in the Arabian Peninsula, continued to plan strikes against the United States.

The terrorist network "suffered several significant setbacks in 2009 due to Pakistani military operations aimed at eliminating militant strongholds, leadership losses, and increased difficulty in raising money, training recruits, and planning attacks outside of the region," the department said.

"Al-Qaeda continued its efforts to encourage key regional affiliates and terrorist networks to pursue a global agenda, using both the Internet as a means to distribute propaganda and telecommunications infrastructure to plan attacks and coordinate movements," the release says. "Going forward, this will be an area of continued focus for the United States" (US State Department release, August 5, 2010).

There were 10,999 terrorist strikes around the world in 2009 that killed 14,971 people, the State Department found. That number, however, was the lowest in five years. The deadliest year for terrorist attacks in that period was 2006 which saw 14,443 strikes that killed 22,736 individuals, according to the report.

Cuba, Iran, Sudan and Syria were all cited as state sponsors of terrorism, with Tehran accused of being the leading backer of militant extremist groups, according to a Defense Department release. Extremist groups were also active in Afghanistan, Iraq, Lebanon, Pakistan, Somalia, Yemen and elsewhere, according to the report (US Defense Department release, August 5, 2010).

Periodical and Internet Sources Bibliography

The following articles have been selected to supplement the diverse views presented in this chapter.

Katherine Charlet, "The New Killer Pathogens: Countering the Coming Bioweapons Threat," Carnegie Endowment for International Peace, April 17, 2018. https://carnegieendowment. org/2018/04/17/new-killer-pathogens-countering-coming-bioweapons-threat-pub-76009.

Simon Cooper, "North Korea's Biochemical Threat," *Popular Mechanics*, September 30, 2009. https://www.popularmechanics. com/military/a1174/4208958/.

Sami Ghanmi, "New Biological Weapons Could Emerge From Today's Technology: Here's How That Could Happen," *Tech Times*, June 20, 2018. https://www.techtimes.com/articles/230713/20180620/ new-biological-weapons-could-emerge-from-today-s-technology-here-s-how-that-might-happen.htm.

Carole N. House, "The Chemical, Biological, Radiological, and Nuclear Terrorism Threat from the Islamic State," *Military Review*, September/October 2016. https://www.armyupress.army. mil/Special-Topics/Hot-Topics/Countering-WMD-CWMD-Operations/.

Yaron Steinbuch, "North Korea's Next Move: Biological Warfare," *New York Post*, December 11, 2017. https://nypost.com/2017/12/11/ north-koreas-next-step-biological-warfare/.

Loren Thompson, "The Threat of Biological Warfare is Increasing, and the US Isn't Ready," *Forbes*, April 9, 2018. https://www.forbes. com/sites/lorenthompson/2018/04/09/biowar-a-guide-to-the-coming-plague-years/#218cf9a85fe5.

Lydia Zuraw, "The Plague is Back: The Bioweapon of Choice," *Independent*, January 11, 2017. https://www.independent.co.uk/ life-style/health-and-families/the-plague-is-back-the-bioweapon-of-choice-a7505996.html.

CHAPTER 4

The Future of Chemical and Biological Warfare

In the United States Improvements to Infrastructure Are Needed to Prevent Bioterrorism

Margaret A. Hamburg

In the following viewpoint, Margaret A. Hamburg analyzes the complex issue of bioterrorism. Hamburg focuses on the forms an attack may take and what medical personnel might be on the front lines of service to those afflicted. Hamburg details what the United States must do to prepare for a response to an attack, or to possibly prevent such an incident. Dr. Margaret A. Hamburg is the Foreign Secretary of the National Academy of Medicine, which partners with the National Academy of Science, Engineering and Medicine.

As you read, consider the following questions:

1. Who would be the first responders in the case of a bioterrorism attack according to Hamburg?
2. How might bioterrorism diseases be better detected according to Hamburg?
3. Which US government agency is charged with dealing with the threat and response to bioterrorism?

Reprinted with permission from ISSUES IN SCIENCE AND TECHNOLOGY, Hamburg, "Preparing for and Preventing Bioterrorism," Winter 2002, p. 27-30, by the University of Texas at Dallas, Richardson, TX.

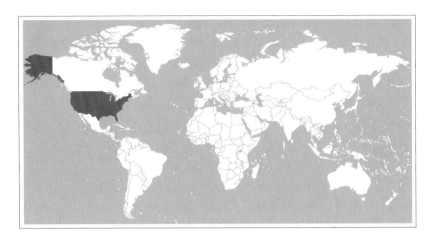

S trengthening the US public health infrastructure is the key to enhancing the nation's safety.

The tragic events of September 11th, followed by the recent anthrax incidents, have made us painfully aware of our nation's vulnerability to terrorism, including bioterrorism. Although once considered a remote concern, the possibility that a biological agent might be intentionally used to cause widespread panic, disease, and death is now a common concern. Whether the event involves an unsophisticated delivery system with a limited number of true cases, as we have seen with the current anthrax scare, or a carefully orchestrated attack with mass casualties, the prospects are frightening. As the United States mobilizes to address an array of overlapping foreign policy, infectious disease, and national security threats, it must make sure that a comprehensive program to counter and prevent bioterrorism ranks high on the priority list.

The threat of bioterrorism is fundamentally different from other threats we face, such as conventional explosives or even a chemical or nuclear weapon. By its very nature, the bioweapons threat, with its close links to naturally occurring infectious agents and disease, requires a different strategy. Meaningful progress against this threat depends on understanding it in the context of epidemic disease. It requires different investments and different partners. Without this recognition, the nation's preparedness programs will be inadequate, and we may miss critical opportunities to prevent such an attack from occurring in the first place.

Biological terrorism is not a "lights and sirens" kind of attack. Unless the release is announced or a fortuitous discovery occurs early on, there will be no discrete event to signal that an attack has happened, and no site that can be cordoned off while authorities take care of the casualties, search for clues, and eventually clean up and repair the damage. Instead, a bioterrorism event would most likely unfold as a disease epidemic, spread out in time and place before authorities even recognize that an attack has occurred. Recognition that an attack had occurred would emerge only when people began appearing in their doctor's office or an emergency room with unusual symptoms or inexplicable disease. In fact, it may prove difficult to ever identify the perpetrators or the site of release—or even to determine whether the disease outbreak was intentional or naturally occurring.

The first responders to a bioterroism event would be public health officials and health care workers. Unfortunately, in many scenarios, diagnosis of the problem may be delayed, because medical providers and labs are not equipped to recognize and deal with the disease agents of greatest concern. What is more, effective medical interventions may be limited, and where they exist, the window of opportunity for successful intervention would be narrow. The outbreak is likely to persist over a prolonged period—months to years—because of disease contagion or continuing exposure. The speed of recognition and response to an attack will be pivotal in reducing casualties and controlling disease.

Not only are biological weapons capable of causing extraordinary devastation, but they are relatively easy to produce, inexpensive, and capable of causing significant damage even when small quantities are delivered by simple means. In addition, information about how to obtain and prepare bioweapons is increasingly available through the Internet, the open scientific literature, and other sources. Opportunities for access to dangerous pathogens can be fairly routine; some of these organisms are commonly found in nature or are the subject of legitimate study in government, academic, and industry labs. Furthermore, bioweapons facilities can be hidden within legitimate research laboratories or pharmaceutical manufacturing sites.

Developing a Response

Although there are enormous challenges before us, many of the elements of a comprehensive approach are relatively straightforward. Some of the necessary activities are already under way, though they may need to be expanded or reconfigured; other programs and policies still need to be developed and implemented.

Perhaps most fundamental to an effective response is the understanding that public health is an important pillar in the national security framework and that public health professionals must be full partners on the US security team. In fact, the president should appoint a public health expert to the National Security Council, and Governor Ridge must include public health experts among his key staff in his new Office of Homeland Security.

Today, experts agree that there is an urgent need to increase the core capacities of the public health system to detect, track, and contain infectious disease. State and local public health departments represent the backbone of our ability to respond effectively to a major outbreak of disease, including a bioterrorist attack. Yet these public health agencies have never been adequately supported or equipped to fulfill this mission. In fact, many hesitate to call the array of health structures at the state, county, and local level a public health "system," because years of relative neglect and underfunding have left them undercapitalized, fragmented, and uncoordinated.

Upgrading current public health capacities will require significantly increased and sustained new investments. First and foremost, this means providing resources to strengthen and extend effective surveillance systems that can rapidly detect and investigate unusual clusters of symptoms or disease. This will entail expanding and strengthening local epidemiologic capabilities, including trained personnel and increasing laboratory capacity to rapidly analyze and identify biological agents. In addition, communication systems, including computer links, must be improved to facilitate collection, analysis, and sharing of information among public health and other officials at local, state, and federal levels. Beyond these critical domestic needs, successful strategies must also include a renewed commitment to improving global public health.

To improve detection, it is essential that physicians and other health care workers be trained to recognize unusual disease or clusters of symptoms that may be manifestations of a bioterroist attack. This must also include strengthening the relationship between medicine and public health so that physicians understand their responsibility to report disease or unusual symptoms to the public health department. Physicians must know whom to call and be confident that their call will contribute to the overall goal of providing information, guidance, and support to the medical community. Health care professional organizations, academic medical institutions, and public health officials must come together to develop appropriate training curricula, informational guidelines, and most important, the working partnerships that are critical to success.

Those same partnerships will be very important in addressing another critical concern: the urgent need to develop emergency plans for a surge of patients in the nation's hospitals. We must enhance systems to support mass medical care and develop innovative strategies to deliver both protective and treatment measures under mass casualty and/or exposure conditions, especially when there may be an additional set of very difficult infection-control requirements as well. This will require careful advance planning since most hospitals are operating at or near capacity right now. Systematic examination of local capabilities and how they can be rapidly augmented by state and federal assets must be part of this effort.

Federal health leadership will be important in this effort to define needs and provide model guidelines and standards; federal resources may also be essential to support planning efforts and to create the incentives necessary to bring the voluntary and private health care sector fully on board. However, the final planning process must be undertaken on the local or regional level, engaging all the essential community partners and capabilities. It is critical to remember that the front line of response, even in a national crisis, is always local. Thus, across all these domains of activity, we must make sure that we have adequate capacity locally and regionally, which can then be supplemented as needed.

Another important example of this involves access to essential drugs and vaccines. A large-scale release of a biological weapon may require rapid access to quantities of antibiotics, vaccines, or antidotes that would not be routinely available in the locations affected. Given that such an attack is a low probability and unpredictable event in any given place, it would hardly be sensible or cost effective to stockpile supplies at the local level.

As we ramp up our public health and medical capacity to respond to bioterrorism, we should continue to strengthen our national pharmaceutical stockpile so that vital drugs and equipment can be rapidly mobilized as needed. The federal Centers for Disease Control and Prevention (CDC) has the responsibility to maintain and oversee use of this stockpile, which currently represents a cache of supplies located in strategic locations across the country that can be delivered within 12 hours to any place in the nation. Current concerns make it clear that the nature and quantities of materials maintained in the stockpile must be enhanced, and the stockpile contents should be periodically reviewed and adjusted in response to intelligence about credible threats. New investments in the stockpile should also include contractual agreements with pharmaceutical manufacturer's to ensure extra production capability for drugs and vaccines in a crisis as well as heightened security at the various storage and dispersal sites.

Beyond simply having the drugs and vaccines available, we must develop plans for how those critical supplies will be distributed to those who need them. [The] CDC needs to provide strong leadership and support for state and local health departments to undertake contingency planning for distribution. We must also think about the broader mobilization of essential drugs, vaccines, or other materials in the event that they are needed outside the United States. Although this may raise complex diplomatic issues, especially when the necessary pharmaceutical is in short supply, addressing potential global need is essential for political and disease-control reasons.

To make sure that the United States can remain strategically poised, further investments must be made in biomedical research to develop new drugs, vaccines, rapid diagnostic tests, and other medical weapons to add to the arsenal against bioterrorism. We must learn more about the fundamental questions of how these organisms cause disease and how the human immune system responds so that we can develop better treatments and disease-containment strategies. It is also essential that we improve technologies to rapidly detect biological agents from environmental samples and develop new strategies and technologies to protect the health of the public.

Scientists will need the full support and encouragement of the public and the government [to] confront this threat. Success will entail research endeavors and collaboration involving numerous government agencies, universities, and private companies. Looking to the future, an effective, well-funded research agenda may give us the tools to render the threat of biological weapons obsolete.

An Ounce of Prevention

Stopping a biological attack before it happens is obviously the most desirable way to avoid a crisis. The first step in blocking the proliferation and use of biological weapons is to significantly bolster our intelligence. The intelligence community could use additional scientific and medical expertise to help enhance the quality of data collection and analysis. This will require greater partnership and trust between the intelligence community, law enforcement, and public health and biomedical science. These disciplines do not routinely work together, and their professional cultures and practices are not easily merged. Nonetheless, greater coordination of effort is very important to our national defense and must be an element of our nation's developing homeland security strategy.

Sadly, we must recognize that the possibility of bioweapons threats emerging from legitimate biological research is certainly real and embedded in the very science and technology that we herald in laboratories around the world. Vigilance is needed to ensure that the tools of modern genomic biology are not used to create new and more dangerous organisms. This is a complex challenge, for no one would want to impede the progress of legitimate and important science. However, we also have a responsibility to face up to a very real set of concerns. With leadership from the scientific community, we must begin to examine what opportunities may exist to constructively reduce this threat.

Related to this, we must continue to reduce access to dangerous pathogens by helping the scientific community improve security and ensure the safe storage and handling of these materials. Over the past five years, new regulations and requirements have tightened access to biological materials from culture collections in the United States and strengthened the government's ability to monitor the shipping and receipt of dangerous pathogens through a registration process, which also requires disclosure of the intended use for the agents. These are important steps, but more can and should be done to assure that our nation's laboratories have adequate oversight of the use and storage of these materials.

International cooperation will be essential to achieving these goals. The safety and control methods developed for domestic [use] must be extended across the globe if they are to make a real and enduring difference. Coupled with this, we should enhance efforts to provide socially useful research opportunities to scientists who had been employed in the Soviet Union's bioweapons program. Many of these scientists are under- or unemployed, and it is in our interest to see that economic need does not drive them to peddle their knowledge to potential terrorists. We must also support efforts to help them secure or destroy potentially dangerous materials. The US government has supported such efforts through the Cooperative Threat Reduction (CTR) program, but these programs desperately need to be strengthened and expanded. Opportunities to extend the reach of the program to include university and industry R&D collaborations will also be essential to long-term success.

In the final analysis, it may prove impossible to prevent future bioweapons attacks from occurring, but planning and preparation could greatly mitigate the death and suffering that would result. As a nation, we need comprehensive, integrated planning for how we will address the threat of bioterrorism, focusing both on prevention and response. We need to define the relative roles and responsibilities of the different agencies involved, and identify the mechanisms by which the various levels of government will interact and work together. The new Office of Homeland Security is well situated to take on this task. Congress and the president must give this office the resources and authority necessary to develop and implement protective measures. Likewise, federal officials must vigorously pursue international cooperation in this effort.

The United States has always been willing to meet the requirements and pay the bills when it came to our defense systems and security needs. We must now be willing to do the same when it comes to funding critical public health needs. Public health has too often received short shrift in our planning and public funding. This must change. Congress and the public need to understand that strengthening disease surveillance, improving medical consequence management, and supporting fundamental and applied research will be essential in responding to a biological weapons attack in this nation or anywhere in the world. These investments will also enhance our efforts to protect the health and safety of the public from naturally occurring disease. We have a chance to defend the nation against its adversaries and improve the public health system with the same steps. We cannot afford not to do this.

Is It Possible to Control or Regulate the Weaponization of Biology?

Filippa Lentzos

In the following viewpoint, Filippa Lentzos analyzes the role of biological science in the arena of US military preparedness and the possible negative effects of biological research. Lentzos contends that security and science must go hand-in-hand, including a review of scientific and technological research before the findings are published in easily obtained scientific journals. Filippa Lentzos is a senior research fellow in the departments of Global Health and Social Medicine and War Studies at King's College in London.

As you read, consider the following questions:

1. As discussed in the viewpoint, what is the concept of synthetic biology?
2. What is the danger of developing Horsepox virus in the lab according to Lentzos?
3. According to the author, how should security policy and science policy work together?

N o military wishes for an enemy with capabilities that match its own. Indeed, the US chairman of the joint chiefs of staff has said he does not want American service members to ever have to face a fair fight. But how do you stay ahead of an adversary? The United States tries to remain "overmatched"

"How Do We Control Dangerous Biological Research?" by Filippa Lentzos, *Bulletin of the Atomic Scientists*, April 12, 2018. Reprinted by permission.

against any enemy by investing heavily in technological innovation, and today, a considerable part of that investment goes into the biological sciences.

At DARPA—the Defense Advanced Research Projects Agency, the US military's research wing—the goal to "harness biology as technology" is one of four main areas of focus for its strategic investments. The biological sciences are expected to play a significant role in future conflicts and hybrid warfare, and techniques to sequence, synthesize, and manipulate genetic material feature prominently in DARPA efforts. While no countries have openly adopted synthetic biology techniques for offensive use, the US intelligence community says they pose a threat to national security, and a National Academy of Sciences committee, funded by the US Defense Department to systematically assess synthetic biology threats, said that "it is possible to imagine an almost limitless number of potential malevolent uses for synthetic biology." The United States is clearly worried an adversary may be harnessing these methods, and is investing in defensive capabilities. "The same tools of synthetic biology that we're concerned about as being capable of being used against us, we are also using in the laboratories to help develop countermeasures," said Arthur T. Hopkins, acting assistant secretary of defense for nuclear, chemical, and biological defense programs, in Congressional testimony last year.

Russia, too, is concerned an adversary may be harnessing synthetic biology for offensive use. Back in 2012, President Vladimir Putin highlighted "genetic weapons" as a future threat, and last year he claimed that the US military is now secretly collecting Russian biological material.

Washington, Moscow, and other governments say they are focused only on "defensive" biosecurity activities, but there is a fine line between "defensive" and "offensive" in this realm, and the alarming military focus on synthetic biology may cause people to wonder if there is some way to control the weaponization of biology. In fact, the Biological Weapons Convention (BWC) was established back in 1972 to do just that. It has 180 states party, including Russia and the United States, and it unequivocally prohibits the development of biological agents—whether naturally occurring, genetically modified, or chemically synthesized—for the purpose of deliberately causing disease, death, or disruption to the human body's functions.

The BWC, though, is not well equipped to deal with potential security implications of rapidly developing biological research, in part for reasons going back to when it was established. In the tech world, "research and development" are often mentioned in the same breath, but in fact they are distinct, and the convention only addresses one of them. It explicitly bans "development," but is much vaguer when it comes to research activities. There is a reason for this. Those negotiating the treaty in the late 1960s and early 1970s were aware that some early-stage biological research could have multiple uses: that it might lead to positive breakthroughs for human health, or to defensive countermeasures, or to discoveries with significant potential for offensive misuse. In an effort to avoid having to determine exactly what kind of research would and would not be permitted under the treaty, the negotiators addressed only the post-research phase of discovery, that is, efforts to actually develop, manufacture, or acquire biological weapons. It is much harder to prohibit research than manufacturing, and negotiators did not want to get mired in discussions on how to identify and manage particular subsets of research. So they put the topic aside.

With current advances in biology, we can't afford to avoid the topic any longer. It is high time the international community turn its focus to the security and governance of biological research. This is an urgent issue, because whenever a proof of concept, technological breakthrough, or scientific game changer is found to have unexpected military utility, it can significantly alter the balance of incentives and disincentives to comply with BWC obligations. The question is, how do we guard against experiments or lines of inquiry that lead some researchers to pursue the kind of edge that contravenes international norms and legal frameworks?

Both security policy and science policy play a role. Clearly there is not one simple answer. Part of the work has to be done by governments and policymakers focused on international security, and should include strengthening norms against misuse and supporting humanitarian policies; modernizing the BWC to counter its growing irrelevance; increasing capacities to defend against and investigate allegations of misuse; and building transparency, confidence, and trust in biodefence programs. But there is likewise much work that should be done by governments and policymakers in terms of science policy to raise awareness of the security dimension of biological and life-science research, promote research integrity, foster a culture of responsibility, and develop sound accountability practices.

To accomplish any of this, we have to be able to both characterize and evaluate biological research with high misuse potential. This is exceptionally difficult to do, and continues to elude both the international community and national policymakers. The United States has come farther than most countries in its deliberations, and in 2012 began implementing "Dual Use Research of Concern" (DURC) policies after a challenging, decade-long process. These policies establish procedures for reviewing certain types of research with certain types of high-consequence pathogens and toxins. Unfortunately, they contain significant weaknesses, many of which are highlighted by a recent experiment to synthesize horsepox virus from scratch, the details of which have gradually been coming out over the last few months.

The experiment was primarily a proof-of-concept study, carried out in 2016 by virologist David Evans' team at the University of Alberta in Canada and funded by Tonix, a pharmaceutical company headquartered in New York City. Their aim was to demonstrate that it is possible to synthetically create horsepox virus in the lab, and by extension, in the longer-term, that it would be possible to develop a horsepox-based vaccine against smallpox that would be safer and more effective than contemporary vaccines. To do this, the research team obtained gene fragments through mail order from a DNA synthesis company, assembled the fragments into the sequence of the horsepox virus genome, and stitched them together. The resulting virus was then shown to be capable of infecting cells and reproducing.

Evans first discussed the experiment at a World Health Organization (WHO) meeting in November 2016. A Tonix press release came out in March 2017, a report of the WHO meeting was published in May 2017, and the journal Science brought the story to wider prominence in July 2017. A write-up of the study was rejected by two leading science journals before it was eventually published by the journal *PLOS One* in January 2018.

The security concerns raised by the experiment are fairly straightforward. Horsepox virus does not cause disease in humans and is not itself considered a dangerous virus; it is not believed to exist naturally anymore, and the only known samples are stored at the US Centers for Disease Control and Prevention (which, incidentally, would not give Evans' team permission to use them commercially). What classifies the experiment as "of concern," however, is that the proof of concept and methodology for synthetically constructing horsepox virus is equally applicable to horsepox's much more dangerous cousin: the variola virus which causes smallpox. This highly contagious and lethal human disease was eradicated 40 years ago through an extensive global campaign. Existing strains of the variola virus are kept at two WHO high-security labs, and there are ongoing efforts to agree on their destruction and bid a final goodbye to the virus. The horsepox experiment is a step in the wrong direction, actively increasing the likelihood that smallpox could reemerge as a threat to global health security.

The horsepox experiment highlighted three weaknesses in the American DURC policies. First, horsepox virus is not listed as a pathogen requiring review, so the horsepox experiment did not have to be assessed by Evans' team or their institution for potential security concerns before it was carried out. Second, even if the horsepox virus had been listed, the experiment would not be covered by DURC policies, because review obligations only apply to US government-funded research and the horsepox experiment was privately funded.

Yet, while both government and funder review failed, a third "line of defense" did go ahead: publisher review. The PLOS Dual Use Research of Concern Committee reviewed the paper for security concerns and found that the benefits of publication outweighed the risks. Following publication, once the larger biosecurity community had access to the details of the case, a number of experts weighed in on the risk-benefit analysis, arguing that the PLOS committee got it wrong and that there was a weak scientific foundation and even weaker business case for the project. The expert assessments underscore the DURC policies' third weakness: They do not call for collective decision making. This leaves biosecurity research vulnerable to what has been dubbed the "unilateralist's curse," a set of incentives that mean research with high potential for misuse is more likely to be carried out when scientists act independently than when they agree to a decision as a group. Biotechnology researcher Gregory Lewis explains: "Imagine that 100 scientists are individually deciding whether it would be a good idea to synthesize horsepox. All of them act impartially and in good faith: They would only conduct this work if they really thought it was on balance good for humankind. Each of them independently weighs up the risks and benefits of synthesizing horsepox, decides whether it is wise to do so, and acts accordingly … if synthesis of horsepox is not to occur, all 100 scientists must independently decide not to pursue it; while if any of the scientists judges the benefits to outweigh the risks, he or she acts unilaterally to synthesize horsepox." The problem with the DURC policies is that decisions on pursuing potentially harmful research are primarily left to individual researchers and are therefore held hostage to the judgement of the most extreme outlier rather than based on a collectively negotiated group judgment.

Risk-benefit analysis is the wrong approach to biosecurity review. The horsepox situation is symptomatic of a larger problem with DURC policies. Their underlying framework is one of risk-benefit analysis. Quantifying risks and benefits, and weighing them up as equal units of comparison, however, relies on certainty. Yet the security and public health implications of developments in synthetic biology, and of novel bio-technologies more generally, are anything but certain. They are most often vague and unclear. It would therefore be careless to wait for definitive proof of harm before taking any protective action. Good security rests not on evaluating risks and benefits, but rather on managing uncertainty, ambiguity, and ignorance—sometimes even situations where we don't know what we don't know. Standard risk-benefit calculations are the wrong approach to evaluating biological research with high misuse potential.

Security review of biological research requires a different logic. Those at risk should not be required to demonstrate that a given experiment or line of inquiry is potentially dangerous. Rather, the funders who support research, the scientists who conduct it, and the publishers who approve and communicate it should be required to prove the absence of danger. This is the notion behind the maxim "first do no harm" that is fundamental to doctors, and the precautionary principle that many regulatory bodies have applied to new areas of scientific research.

In essence, this principal recognizes that it may be better to do nothing than to risk causing more harm than good. Rather than having decisions that may affect society as a whole made by an individual or a small group of likeminded peers, a regulatory framework controlling dangerous biological research should emphasize collective and transparent decision-making. Such a framework should also encourage exploring alternatives to potentially harmful actions and setting goals that protect health and the environment. We need responsible research and innovation, which continually works to align with the values, needs, and expectations of society.

Guarding against deliberate misuse of biology is a tall order for the international community and national policymakers. On the other hand, it is not an impossible task given political will. We already have frameworks, concepts, and experiences to draw on, including the Biological Weapons Convention and US policies on Dual Use Research of Concern. We can build on these to reduce the security risk posed by the rapid evolution of biology.

Will Syria Continue to Use Chemical Weapons?

Paul B. Stares

In the following viewpoint, Paul B. Stares argues that Syria is not showing signs of discontinuing its chemical weapons strikes. Stares maintains that Syria has an assortment of chemical weapons and might be in danger of having unauthorized field use under certain conditions. Stares also outlines ways to possible prevention of weapon use. Paul B. Stares is the director at the Center for Preventive Action and an expert in the fields of war and conflict, defense and security, and North Korea.

As you read, consider the following questions:

1. What types of chemical weapons are believed to be in the possession of Syria according to Stares?
2. What might cause unauthorized use of chemical weapons in Syria?
3. As explained in the viewpoint, which third party countries should work to contain and prevent chemical weapons use in Syria?

Warnings by the United States and other countries threatening the Syrian regime with dire consequences if chemical weapons are used against rebel forces may have had the intended effect. Recent media reports suggest this concern has

"Preventing Chemical Weapons Use in Syria," by Paul B. Stares, Council on Foreign Relations, December 19, 2012. Reprinted by permission.

now diminished. It is just as plausible, however, that the regime had little intention of using its chemical weapons but fabricated the preparations that prompted the warnings to deter outside intervention in Syria's civil war.

Either way, it is wrong to assume the danger of chemical weapons use in Syria is receding. Indeed, there are good reasons to believe it could grow in the coming weeks and months.

Syria, which is not a signatory of the Chemical Weapons Convention, is widely believed to possess sizeable stocks of different kinds of chemical weapons (CRS)—principally nerve (Sarin, VX) and blister (mustard gas) agents—that have been weaponized into bombs, artillery shells, and possibly warheads for delivery by missiles. How quickly this arsenal could be employed today is unclear from public reports, but it is prudent to believe that some, if not all of it, is operationally ready. Although the fighting to date has more than demonstrated the lethality of conventional weapons, the use of chemical agents would represent a significant escalation of the violence with potentially mass casualty consequences. It would also breach an international norm against the use of chemical weapons that is important to maintain.

Deliberate use of chemical weapons by government forces against either rebel groups or population centers considered sympathetic to their cause is certainly the scenario that has attracted the most concern. But it is just one of many conceivable scenarios to worry about.

For example, should rebel forces progressively gain the upper hand—as they seem to be doing—the regime or elements of the regime might retreat to predominantly Alawite areas of Syria to create a rump state. Chemical weapons could eventually be employed to deter further encroachment or defend these areas when they are assaulted. And if defeat looked inevitable, their use as a final act of defiance cannot be discounted.

Destruction of Chemical Weapons

A State Party can select and implement the appropriate destruction technologies for its chemical weapons by which chemicals are converted in an essentially irreversible way to a form unsuitable for production of chemical weapons and which—in an irreversible manner—renders munitions and other devices unusable as such. A chemical agent, for example, can be neutralised or incinerated, while unfilled munitions and other devices can simply be cut apart.

The Convention also requires States Parties to assign the highest priority to ensuring the safety of people and to protecting the environment during the implementation of its obligation. The methods employed must comply with national and international safety and emissions regulations, and cannot include open-pit burning, land burial, or dumping in any body of water.

Destruction Technologies

Chemical weapons destruction technologies have been developed to destroy assembled unitary chemical weapons (e.g., artillery projectiles, mortars, air bombs, rockets, rocket warheads, spray tanks), bulk chemical weapons agents, binary munitions and recovered chemical weapons munitions.

These technologies can be divided in two main groups:
- high temperature destruction technologies like plasma pyrolysis, incineration and explosion chambers, with the associated off-gas treatment system;

Leaky Weapons

The United States and its international partners cannot assume, moreover, that they know of all the chemical weapons storage sites in Syria or that the movement of munitions from the known ones will be detected in a timely manner. Some may already have been secreted away by the regime as Muammar el-Qaddafi reportedly did after Libya had agreed to destroy its stockpile of chemical weapons.

Maintaining tight command and control over units and personnel with access to chemical weapons will also become increasingly difficult as the regime collapses. For those in the

- low-temperature destruction technologies like neutralisation (i.e., using neutralising agents or a decontamination solution such as monoethanolamine, RD-4M or aqueous NaOH) and hydrolysis followed by secondary treatments of the resulting by-products (i.e., effluent, reaction mass or hydrolysate) like bituminisation (encapsulation), biodegradation or supercritical water oxidation, prior to final disposal in accordance to national regulatory provisions.

Post-treatment of the generated reaction masses that contain Schedule 2b chemicals is also required and done either by incineration, bio-treatment, or supercritical water oxidation.

Verifying Destruction

All destruction activities undertaken by Member States are required to occur under the watchful eye of the OPCW. The goal of verification activities is to confirm the complete destruction of chemical weapons, to provide confidence to States Parties regarding the integrity of the destruction process and the facility as a whole, and to ensure the non-diversion of chemical weapons.

Once completed, the State Party certifies, no later than 30 days after the destruction process has been completed, that all chemical weapons declared have been destroyed. In return, the Technical Secretariat confirms the State Parties declaration—reporting the completion of destruction of the designated quantity of chemical weapons.

"Destruction of Chemical Weapons", OPCW.

field, any ambiguity about who is in charge and in the chain of command heightens the prospect of unauthorized use. Whether there is some pre-delegated authority to use these weapons under certain circumstances is also something to be concerned about.

Another set of worrisome contingencies involve the capture and potential use of chemical weapons stocks by rebel forces. It is not hard to imagine how, in the heat of battle, chemical weapons could be turned against government forces or used in retribution for past atrocities. Some might even see their use as a way to trigger outside intervention. Other wildcard possibilities involve terrorist groups like Hezbollah acquiring chemical weapons in various ways as the Syrian regime crumbles.

Preventing these various threats from materializing clearly represents a much harder challenge than issuing warnings to the Syrian government. A broader, more nuanced strategy is required.

Though not conceived with potential chemical weapons use in mind, the elements of such a strategy can be found in the final report of the Genocide Prevention Task Force, co-chaired by former US secretary of state Madeleine Albright and former US secretary of defense William Cohen. Their report advocated targeting each of the principal groups in any given atrocity situation with a tailored set of preventive measures.

Preventive Steps

In the context of Syria, these target groups would be: those in a position to authorize the use of chemical weapons; those in physical control of them and able to execute orders; the potential victims of their use; and various third parties. The following measures should be considered by the principal international actors concerned by the potential use or loss of chemical weapons in Syria:

- Warnings. In the event the Assad regime begins to unravel, US officials as well as leading North Atlantic Treaty Organization allies and the United Nations secretary-general can reiterate public warnings of the consequences of using chemical weapons and, moreover, bolster these with more explicit threats. These can also be complemented with private messaging to leading figures in the regime that underscores the general warnings with more specific threats of punitive action, including likely criminal indictment.

- Securing loose weapons. Known representatives of rebel groups operating in Syria can be given instructions about securing, if not disabling, chemical weapons stocks that fall into their possession while also being warned of the consequences should their fighters use them. At the same time, consideration should be given to offering inducements, including financial rewards, to rebel forces for supporting this effort. Governments known to be backing other groups with weapons and financial assistance can also be tapped to transmit the same message. These governments could likewise be warned of potential penalties if their proxies use chemical weapons.

- Information warfare. To the extent that government units guarding or capable of using chemical weapons can be identified, these too can be the target of a discrete information warfare campaign. This could include television and radio broadcasts, email messaging (as was apparently used by US forces in the lead up to the invasion of Iraq in 2003), and leafleting known storage sites in a collective effort to dissuade military personnel from using chemical weapons. Again, the messaging can be a mixture of positive and negative inducements to elicit cooperation.

- Military strikes. Military options to deny or preempt the use of chemical weapons by any actor can be readied for rapid execution on receipt of compelling early warning. These range from the use of air strikes (including drones) and special operations forces to cyberattacks. Rebel groups in the vicinity of an expected attack might conceivably be employed to interdict use. Each of these options has different operational implications in terms of speed of use, potential effectiveness, and placing US service personnel in harm's way.

- Surviving an attack. Unless there is accurate forewarning of intentions and preparations to use chemical weapons, the options to help vulnerable populations either avoid or survive an attack are limited. Some basic survival information could conceivably be transmitted to rebel groups to disseminate among local communities. Warnings might also be broadcast through various channels to specific areas deemed at risk but the potential unintended consequence of this could be to instigate mass panic that makes the situation worse.

- Third party interventions. In addition to rebel supporters, there are several critical third parties that can be used to reinforce messaging on chemical weapons by the United States and others. This includes those with long-standing contacts with the Syrian regime (Russia and Iran), and Hezbollah (Iran). Other neighboring countries can be supported to improve their border security against the possible transfer of chemical weapons. And finally, various UN bodies and regional organizations in the Middle East can be encouraged to stress concerns already expressed by the UN secretary-general.

Collectively, these efforts would not preclude the use of chemical weapons in Syria, but they would lessen the risk. Moreover, they should not be a substitute for additional measures in the event these preventive efforts fail. These include additional diplomatic initiatives and potential military measures to disrupt or deter further chemical weapons use in Syria, as well as humanitarian assistance to help affected areas and respond to the possibility of large-scale refugee flows.

In Syria a Chemical Weapons Attack Prompts US Airstrikes

Mika Hayashi

In the following viewpoint, Mika Hayashi analyzes the international response that occurred after the US decision to strike a Syrian military airbase. According to Hayashi, the United States acted after Syria used chemical weapons during an attack on Khan Shaykhyun. Hayashi outlines the response from other world countries and international organizations after the US action. Professor Mika Hayashi teaches at Kobe University in the Graduate School of International Cooperation Studies.

As you read, consider the following questions:

1. As stated in the viewpoint, what reason did the United States give for pursuing airstrikes against Syria?
2. Why did Germany, Italy, and the United Kingdom back up the United States according to Hayashi?
3. Was the action by Syria a war crime as explained in the viewpoint?

The chemical attack in Khan Shaykhun, Syria, reported on April 4, 2017, produced 86 deaths and more than 300 injuries according to the initial reports.[1] The Fact-Finding Mission of the Organisation for the Prohibition of Chemical Weapons

"The U.S. Airstrike After the Use of Chemical Weapons in Syria: National Interest, Humanitarian Intervention, or Enforcement Against War Crimes?" by Mika Hayashi, The American Society of International Law, July 13, 2017. Reprinted by permission.

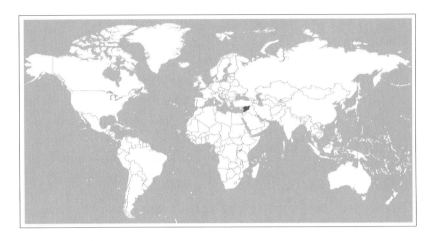

(OPCW) was able to deploy in less than twenty-four hours, and later confirmed the incident,[2] even though Syria "categorically reject[ed] the false accusations and allegations of the Syrian Arab Army's use of toxic chemical substances against Syrian civilians in Khan Shaykhun."[3] In response to this chemical attack, a total of fifty-nine cruise missiles were launched from two US naval vessels, targeting the Al-Shayrat military airbase, which according to the United States, had been used for the chemical attack by the Syrian government that had taken place three days earlier.[4] The UN Security Council that met immediately after the chemical attack had made no decision to authorize the use of force.[5]

The legal assessment of such a response is not immediately clear. On the one hand, there is a growing consensus on the illegality of the use of chemical weapons.[6] On the other hand, that does not automatically make a unilateral military intervention in response [to] a lawful action. Given the prohibition of the use of force under the UN Charter and the narrow and limited exceptions it sets out, it is crucial that clear justifications be offered by the state carrying out a military intervention, and that such justifications be accepted by the international community. In respect to the Syria events, the United States and the states that chose not to criticize the US airstrikes rooted their positions in different legal theories. This *Insight* examines how states responded, focusing on three types of justification: self-defense, humanitarian intervention, and enforcement against war crimes.

Could the US airstrike on April 7, 2017, be justified as the exercise of right to self-defence, as the action was said to be in the "vital national security interest" of the United States?[7] According to the US president and his spokesperson, the idea behind this justification was that leaving the situation in Syria unattended produced a prospect or possibility of proliferation of chemical weapons and/or that these weapons may be directed at the United States at some point in the future: "The reason that we took action was multifold—number one, to stop the proliferation and deterrence of chemical weapons. When you see mass weapons of destruction being used it should be a concern to every nation, especially our own people. The proliferation of those weapons pose [sic] a grave threat to our national security. So, number one, we have to stop that."[8] This resonates with what the United States had advanced as a reason for a military intervention in 2013.[9]

However, self-defense is conditional upon the existence of an imminent threat. The perceived threat of proliferation, or an eventual attack on the United States, can hardly be construed as an imminent threat as required by the conventional doctrine of self-defense or by Article 51 of the UN Charter. Presenting a remote future scenario as a threat in the context of right to self-defense proved to be very controversial, as the debate about the preemptive doctrine in the past vividly illustrates.[10]

What is striking in the present case, though, is that the majority of states that chose not to criticize the US airstrike appear to be uninterested in this line of argument. Indeed, very few states even refer to the US "vital national security interest" in the form of the prevention of chemical weapons' proliferation as the reason for accepting the US airstrike.[11] On the whole, the threat of proliferation as a justification is not selling.

The second line of argument is humanitarian intervention. The US airstrike has also been described by the White House spokesperson as "a clear response on humanitarian purposes,"[12] and the message by the US president cited previously[13] indicates that a humanitarian concern had a significant role in the decision to carry out the airstrike. This notion that the scale of the humanitarian distress caused by the chemical attack justified, at least partially, the US airstrike found much more purchase in the reactions of other states. For example, instead of condemning the airstrike, the German Chancellor stated that the US airstrike was "understandable" given, among other factors, the suffering of innocent people.[14] The Italian foreign minister was of a similar view.[15] The United Kingdom stated in a Security Council meeting that the airstrike was a response "to unspeakable acts that gave rise to overwhelming humanitarian distress."[16]

While none of these statements and remarks, including those of the United States, explicitly refer to humanitarian intervention as a legal doctrine and justification, the doctrine is the only legal language currently available that can accommodate the expressed sentiments. Moreover, humanitarian intervention was raised as a possible justification by the United Kingdom in 2013[17] when it was considering a possible military intervention because of the chemical attack in Ghouta, Syria.

However, the doctrine of humanitarian intervention cannot be upheld as a rule of positive law lightly. It remains very controversial as a doctrine to give lawful cover to a unilateral military intervention without the Security Council's authorization in the case of overwhelming humanitarian distress.[18]

In the Syria situation, there appears to be a third, emerging idea that made the US airstrike acceptable to other states: the enforcement of international law in the face of a violated rule. A short survey of remarks by states and other international actors indicates that the US airstrike was accepted or endorsed as a form of enforcement of the rule prohibiting the use of chemical weapons. In support of the US airstrike, the president of the EU Commission stated that "the repeated use of such weapons must be answered" and that the US airstrikes "seek to deter further chemical weapons atrocities."[19] The statement of the NATO

Secretary-General immediately after the airstrike also stressed that "any use of chemical weapons is unacceptable, cannot go unanswered, and those responsible must be held accountable."[20] The joint communiqué issued by France and Germany on the same day also supported the US airstrike, emphasizing that the "continued recourse to chemical weapons and mass crimes cannot remain unpunished."[21] The British Permanent Representative to the UN stated that "the United Kingdom supports the US air strike on the Al Shayrat airfield because war crimes have consequences."[22]

Such a justification for the US airstrike does not, of course, signal a general acceptance of unilateral enforcement against any violation of any rule. The first important qualification, recurrent and consistent in various statements in the present case, is that this airstrike was a measure against a war crime, or a crime of such gravity that it cannot be left unattended. The second qualification, again fairly consistent across various statements, is that this particular unilateral measure was, and must remain, an interim measure pending a resolution in a multilateral framework, in particular at the United Nations.

The idea that an airstrike can be lawful when construed as an enforcement measure against a war crime also raises fresh questions. Viewed as a sign of an emerging international consensus, the present case is intriguing because the United States did not put it forward. It is those who reacted to the US airstrike that expressed this idea. In the doctrine of customary international law, state practice and opinio juris as the evidence of customary rule are supposed to be concomitant. From that perspective, it may be peculiar to view the present case as part of a rule formation. States commenting on the US actions appear to be providing an opinio juris, while the state that acted, the United States, is providing evidence of state practice without explicitly sharing the same opinio juris. Nevertheless, it would seem that if the state that acts does not express any subsequent view that contradicts opinio juris expressed by the commenting states, the agglomeration of opinio juris and state practice in this situation may bolster the case for a rule formation. Needless to say, the remaining conditions in the traditional customary international law doctrine must be met in order to argue that there is in fact a customary rule.

There is also a technical but important question regarding the use of the term "war crime." Was it merely a rhetorical device, or did states truly mean that the use of chemical weapons in a non-international conflict, such as their use by the Syrian armed forces in the present case, is a war crime under international law? In this regard, the amendment to the ICC Statute adopted by consensus in 2010 included the addition of the use of chemical weapons to the list of war crimes under Article 8(2)e.[23] This may amount to evidence that at least eighty-four states were inclined to view the prohibited use of chemical weapons in a non-international armed conflict as a war crime.

In conclusion, none of the three theories explored as justifications for a military intervention garnered an international consensus in the Syria situation. In the unmistakable presence of divergent views about the case and the rules among various actors, it is certainly not possible to confirm the existence or emergence of a rule allowing a third state to resort to use of force as a response to the prohibited use of chemical weapons in a non-international armed conflict. Given this context, it is all the more important to know what these divergent views were, and to discern the ideas that may lead to an emergence of a new consensus.

Notes

1. The information appears in the *Briefing to the UN Security Council on the Situation in Syria by the Under-Secretary-General for Political Affairs*, UN Dept. for Political Affairs (Apr. 7, 2017). http://www.un.org/undpa/en/speeches-statements/07042017/Middle-East.
2. Ahmet Üzümcü (OPCW Director-General), *Note by the Technical Secretariat: Status Update of the OPCW Fact-finding Mission in Syria Regarding a Reported Incident in Khan Shaykhun*, 4 April 2017. UN Doc. S/2017/440 (May 19, 2017).
3. U.N. SCOR, 72d Sess., 7915 mtg, UN Doc. S/PV.7915 (Apr. 5, 2017) [hereinafter Apr. 5 Security Council Meeting].
4. U.N. SCOR, 72d Sess., 7919 mtg, UN Doc. S/PV.7919 (Apr. 7, 2017) [hereinafter Apr. 7 Security Council Meeting].
5. Apr. 5 Security Council Meeting, supra note 3.

6. Chemical Weapons Convention art. 1, Sept. 3, 1992, 1972 UNTS. 45. For the customary rule prohibiting the use of chemical weapons, see Masahiko Asada, "A Path to a Comprehensive Prohibition of the Use of Chemical Weapons under International Law: From The Hague to Damascus," *J. Conflict & Sec. L.* 153, vol 21 (2016). See also various statements in the Apr. 5 Security Council Meeting, supra note 3.

7. Mythili Sampathkumar, "Syria Missile Strike: Donald Trump's Speech in Full," *The Independent* (Apr. 7, 2017). http://www.independent.co.uk/news/world/americas/us-politics/donald-trump-latest-syria-missile-strike-tomahawk-chemical-weapons-attack-idlib-beautiful-babies-a7671471.html.

8. Daily Press Briefing by Press Secretary Sean Spicer, The White House (Apr. 10, 2017). https://www.whitehouse.gov/the-press-office/2017/04/10/daily-press-briefing-press-secretary-sean-spicer-35.

9. Mika Hayashi, "Reacting to the Use of Chemical Weapons: Options for Third States," *J. on Use of Force & Int'l L.* vol. 1, 110 n.154 (2014) (citing President Obama: "I Have Not Made a Decision" on Syria, PBS (Aug. 28, 2013). http://www.pbs.org/newshour/bb/white_house-july-dec13-obama_08-28/).

10. Id. at 110–12.

11. Japan appears to be the only state among the ones examined below that explicitly sympathized with the US concern for the proliferation of chemical weapons. Comment by Prime Minister Shinzo Abe on the Situation in Syria at a Press Occasion, Prime Minister of Japan and His Cabinet (Apr. 7, 2017). http://japan.kantei.go.jp/97_abe/decisions/2017/press170407.html.

12. Press Gaggle by Press Secretary Sean Spicer, The White House (Apr. 7, 2017). https://www.whitehouse.gov/the-press-office/2017/04/07/press-gaggle-press-secretary-sean-spicer.

13. Sampathkumar, supra note 7.

14. "Assad trägt alleinige Verantwortung" ["Assad Bears Sole Responsibility"], *Die Bundeskanzlerin* [*The Chancellor*] (Apr. 7, 2017). https://www.bundeskanzlerin.de/Content/DE/Artikel/2017/04/2017-04-05-giftgas-in-syrien.html. The German Chancellor also refers to the state of the Security Council on this issue and the continued use of chemical weapons as two other elements that make the US action "understandable."

15. A statement given to the press is also available at the website of the Ministry, Siria [Syria], Ministro degli Affari Esteri e della Cooperazione Internazionale [Ministry of Foreign Affairs and International Cooperation] (Apr. 7, 2017). http://www.esteri.it/mae/it/sala_stampa/archivionotizie/comunicati/2017/04/siria_0.html. The statement of Italy in the Security Council meeting later on the same day confirmed this statement. Apr. 7 Security Council Meeting, supra note 4.

16. Apr. 7 Security Council Meeting, supra note 4.

17. See Hayashi, supra note 9, at 115 n.193.

18. Christine Gray, "The Use of Force for Humanitarian Purposes," in *Research Handbook on International Conflict and Security Law: Jus ad Bellum, Jus in Bello and Jus post Bellum* 231-40 (Nigel D. White & Christian Henderson eds., 2013).

19. European Commission Press Release, Statement by the President of the EU Commission on the Situation in Syria (Apr. 7, 2017). http://europa.eu/rapid/press-release_STATEMENT-17-912_en.htm.

20. Statement by NATO Secretary General Jens Stoltenberg on US Strikes in Syria, NATO (Apr. 7, 2017). http://www.nato.int/cps/en/natohq/news_143082.htm.

21. "Communiqué franco-allemand sur les frappes américaines en Syrie" ["French-German Statement on US Strikes in Syria"], *La France en Allemagne* [*France in Germany*] (Apr. 7, 2017), https://de.ambafrance.org/Communique-franco-allemand-sur-les-frappes-americaines-en-Syrie; and "Gemeinsame Erklärung von Bundeskanzlerin Merkel und Frankreichs Präsident Hollande nach den Luftschlägen in Syrien" ["Joint statement by Chancellor Merkel and France's President Hollande After the Air Strikes in Syria"], *Die Bundeskanzlerin* [*The Chancellor*] (Apr. 7, 2017), https://www.bundeskanzlerin.de/Content/DE/Pressemitteilungen/BPA/2017/04/2017-04-07-erklaerung-merkel-hollande.html.

22. Apr. 7 Security Council Meeting, supra note 4.

23. Amendment to Article 8 of the Rome Statute of the International Criminal Court, June 10, 2010, 2868 U.N.T.S. 195.

A Watchdog Group to Monitor Bioweapons Development Is Essential

Patrick Tucker

In the following viewpoint, Patrick Tucker examines the issue of scientific research and the consequences of emerging technologies in the face of bioweapons production. Tucker's analysis pinpoints the difficulties posed to the scientific community. He demonstrates that even though research is necessary, costs will incur if and when knowledge gets into the wrong hands. Patrick Tucker is the technology editor at Defense One, an online newsletter.

As you read, consider the following questions:

1. According to the viewpoint, what are "gain-of-function" studies?
2. What is the difference between "understanding" and "developing" according to the author?
3. How does RTTA affect scientific research as stated in the viewpoint?

I n June 2012, a team of researchers from the University of Wisconsin published a paper in the journal *Nature* about airborne transmission of H5N1 influenza, or bird flu, in ferrets.

The article changed the way the United States and nations around the world approached manmade biological threats.

This was not the researchers' intent.

The team had altered the virus's amino acid profile, allowing it to reproduce in mammal lungs, which are a bit colder than bird lungs. That small change allowed the virus to be transmitted via coughing and sneezing, and it solved the riddle of how H5N1 could become airborne in humans.

The US government initially supported the work through grants, but members of Congress, among other critics around the world, responded to the publication of the research with alarm and condemnation. A *New York Times* editorial described the experiment and similar research conducted in the Netherlands, eventually published in the journal as "An Engineered Doomsday." So the researchers agreed to a voluntary moratorium on their findings. In October, the White House Office of Science and Technology Policy announced that it would halt funding for research into how to make diseases more lethal—so-called "gain-of-function" studies—and asked anyone doing such research on deadly diseases to cease and desist.

The White House moratorium was not a direct response to the original University of Wisconsin study so much as it was an answer to a series of embarrassing incidents that included improperly handling contaminated wastes, accidentally shipping dangerous pathogens, and "inventory holdovers" at government labs. Nevertheless, the Wisconsin study features prominently in the current discussion within government and labs around the world about the costs and benefits of certain types of scientific inquiry.

Why do research on how to make the world's most dangerous viruses and bugs more lethal? The answer varies tremendously depending on who is asking and for what purpose the research is taking place. While experts differ in their views on how and where such work should be done, there is wide agreement that the barriers to entry for new biological creations, including ones that could kill millions of people, are decreasing.

Today, there is little international enforcement of limitations on bioweapons. For chemical materials like sarin gas, the Chemical Weapons Convention provides a treaty-based legal framework for stopping proliferation, and a watchdog group, the Organization for the Prohibition of Chemical Weapons, to investigate potential violations. No similar watchdog exists around biological weapons. All but a few countries have ratified the Biological and Toxin Weapons Convention, for instance; among the no-shows is Syria, where President Bashar al-Assad's regime is suspected of harboring strains of smallpox for research.

"In light of this, it is indeed Assad's biological weapon complex that poses a far greater threat than his chemical-weapons complex," wrote bioweapons expert Jill Bellamy van Aalst and GlobalStrat managing director Olivier Guitta in *The National Interest* in 2013. Some of the biological research that the Assad regime was conducting was based in Homs, Van Aalst and Guitta wrote, putting smallpox samples or possibly rudimentary bioweapons within reach of the Islamic State, or ISIS.

Dangerous Research and Unknown Unknowns

The genetic engineering of deadly pathogens is not the sort of thing that a terrorist or would-be supervillain could easily attempt in a kitchen. But the quickening pace of genetics research has plenty of scientists worried. Suzanne Fry, director of the Strategic Futures Group at the Office for the Director of National Intelligence, told a group at last month's SXSW technology conference in Austin, Texas, that synthetic biology was a big concern among many of the technologists she's been interviewing recently. "Some very, very prominent scientists have said that that worries them very much," she said.

George Church, a Harvard Medical School researcher widely considered a father of modern genetic research, offered a somber assessment of the future of genetically engineered bioterror. "How would we have calculated the odds of the events on 9-11-2001 on 9-10-2001?" he said via email, "or the Aum Shinrikyo [Tokyo

Fort Detrick

Fort Detrick, Md., was created in the middle of World War II and became the center for America's biological warfare efforts. But that role shifted in 1969, the government says, to focus solely on defense against the threat of biological weapons. Then called Detrick Air Field, the science and research facility housed four biological agent production plants.

During the 1950s, the biological weapons program was among the most classified within the Pentagon. There was an emphasis on biological agents for use against enemy forces as well as plants and animals. The Army says no biological weapons were used during the Korean War, though such allegations were made by the Chinese and the Koreans.

One plan at Fort Detrick in the late 1950s was to use the yellow fever virus against an enemy by releasing infected mosquitoes by airplane or helicopter. Detrick's labs were capable of producing a half-million mosquitoes per month, with plans for up to 130 million per month.

The military also tested bombs in Utah with *Brucella suis*, a bacterium that can lead to fever and influenzalike sickness. And scientists at Fort Detrick also worked on a number of possible pathogens that could destroy crops or trees.

By the 1960s, the US biological warfare program had begun to decline, with funding gradually decreasing. There were growing protests in the United States over the use of defoliants in Vietnam and anger about a sheep-kill incident in Utah. That incident occurred in 1968, when 3,000 sheep were found dead in the Skull Valley area, adjacent to the Army's Dugway Proving Ground. Although the findings were not conclusive, it was believed that nerve agents had somehow drifted out of Dugway during a test of aerial spraying.

In 1969, the Army announced that 23 US soldiers and one US civilian had been exposed to a sarin nerve agent on the Japanese island of Okinawa, while cleaning sarin-filled bombs. The incident created international concerns and revealed that the Army had secretly positioned chemical munitions in Southeast Asia.

That same year, President Nixon took action against biological and chemical weapons. He reaffirmed a no-first-use policy for chemical weapons, renounced the use of biological weapons and limited research to defensive measures only.

"Fort Detrick: From Biowarfare To Biodefense," by Tom Bowman, NPR.org, August 1, 2008.

subway attacks]? Hopefully, before anything happens, the good guys will get better at new pathogen detection and immunity soon—both to prevent this scenario and naturally emerging infectious diseases."

There's a difference between building better detection kits and figuring out how to engineer new and more lethal versions of familiar viruses. But these areas of exploration are not always distinct. The best and most reliable Ebola detection devices work off of the virus's unique genetic signature, giving a level of certainty unmatched by fever scanners and other symptom trackers. A new Ebola-like pathogen with a unique genetic signature might be undetectable to the most up-to-date devices and methods.

The H5N1 case shows how a once-difficult challenge is becoming exponentially easier because published results move so quickly in the age of digital interconnection, according to Gaymon Bennett, an Arizona State University religious studies professor and biotechnology expert who has written extensively on synthetic biology.

"It took specialized facilities and millions of dollars" for University of Wisconsin researchers to figure out how [to] create the amino acid sequence that would allow the virus to reproduce in mammal lungs, he said. "But once you publish the sequences ... once they've done that work, it would take a competent physician a few thousand dollars and few weeks to reproduce the result."

Richard Danzig, a former Navy secretary, says that he understands the impetus towards moratoriums. He points to the years following the Manhattan Project, when research was classified and researchers monitored, as an example of a research control regime that worked. But today, the Internet makes implementing a similar control regime much harder, Danzig said at a 2013 Atlantic Council event. "Our capabilities to control information seem inadequate, so that the distortive effects of those kinds of controls tend to outweigh, I think, the positive effects," he said. "It turns out that the information leaks in a hundred ways or is independently recreated in a global world outside the reach of your jurisdiction."

For the military, the reasons to conduct gain-of-function research may outweigh reasons to suppress it. Military leaders are fond of saying that they don't want to ever find themselves in a fair fight—they always want the advantage. In the context of biological threats, that means understanding how to weaponize Ebola even if international laws and treaties, like the Geneva Convention, prohibit the use of such weapons in the field. Of course "understanding" is different from actually developing a weaponized Ebola strain, which is illegal under the Biological Weapons Convention.

Last year, the Pentagon's Defense Advanced Projects Research Agency, or DARPA, opened a biological technologies office to explore issues such as synthetic biology and epidemiology. Its work includes everything from creating new high-energy density materials from organic matter to exploring how diseases spread and become more dangerous. DARPA Director Arati Prabhakar recently said she created the office because of the rising potency of biotechnology powered by information technology. "When I say I see the seeds of technological surprise in that area, that's exactly what I mean. Hugely powerful technologies are bubbling out of that research."

Prabhakar said the agency constantly considers the political and scientific controversies surrounding biotechnology research, but that it isn't in the interests of DARPA or the nation to hold back because of controversy. "We're responsible to be in those areas but we're also responsible for raising those issues and convening that dialogue. What we've done that's been very helpful is tap experts in different areas. We have experts in neuroethics, other experts who are very smart in synthetic biology and law, policy and societal issues … but DARPA is not going to make up answers to these societal choices. That's a much broader undertaking."

The cheapest and most effective way to do that research is to open it up to more scientists and better publication opportunities. If the US doesn't, someone else might.

"It's a huge dilemma for our military," said Gary Marchant, professor of emerging technologies, law, and ethics at Arizona

State University. He spoke at New America Foundation's Future of War conference in February. (Defense One is a media partner of the foundation's.) "We know that there's going to be people out there who won't follow those same self-imposed restrictions. To understand what those threats are and be able to counter them do we need to make the monster ourselves? And when we do this stuff, do we publish it?"

The problem of how to control bioterror information in the Information Age is complex and important enough to cause a shift in science itself, according to some members of the research and university community. At [the] very least, it's enough to prompt a change in the way in which some scientific research happens.

One of the basic principles of science is the idea that all research conducted in accordance with sound scientific methods—and that does not directly harm any humans or put them at risk—adds value to civilization. Of course, a terrorist or nation-state could use the product of such research to harm innocents. But the potential for misuse should not prevent the research in the first place.

The Wisconsin study has caused some to question the infallibility of that centuries-old approach.

Predicting What Science Will Do Before It Does It

Instead of trying to figure out how to contain potentially dangerous bioterrorism discoveries, one alternative gaining support is trying to predict—or at least try to forecast or model—the outcomes of research before it occurs.

"We've been working on a tool in our consortium of science policy and outcomes where we've been thinking through: How would you think about the implications of a technology at the time that it became scientifically feasible ... not doable but feasible ... how would you think through all of the implications and then guide the evolution of the technology so that you then get these ... unalterable outcomes that could effect the entire species," ASU president Michael Crow said at the Future of War conference.

He envisions that this tool, called Real-Time Technology Assessment, or RTTA, would expand the different inputs that go into the discussion that universities, labs, research communities and individuals have about what research to pursue. Some of the inputs might be social, some technical, some political and so on. Importantly, says Crow, the effect of the assessment would not necessarily be to limit or torpedo any particular effort or give sociologists veto power over what sort of topics chemists pursue. Rather, the intent is to create the fullest picture possible of the total effects of the research. "[Imagine] that we avoid conflict in the future by re-thinking how we do science now. Not taking away the fundamental discovery of aspect."

David Guston, an ASU political science professor, invented the RTTA concept in a seminal paper co-written with Daniel Sarewitz. The authors describe the tool as a system that uses opinion polling, focus groups, and futurist methodologies like scenario planning and socio-technical mapping to explore ways that different people may respond to the scientific or technological innovation under consideration.

RTTA is "about using a fairly traditional set of social science research tools to help create more thoughtful consideration on the part of scientists and engineers of the choices they make in the laboratory," Guston said.

If the process works correctly, the researchers—and everyone who may be harmed or benefit from the research—has a clear and shared understanding of how the technology, innovation, or experiment may change life on this planet, no matter who undertakes it.

Why do we need it?
By way of example, Guston cited some of Church's work: the Harvard researcher recently unveiled a novel strain of *E. coli* bacteria that needs an artificial amino acid to survive, and so the amino acid serves as an on/off switch. The paper that Church co-wrote with several other authors marks a foundational contribution

to the future development of synthetic life forms. It shows one method by which humans can assert control over the survival and reproducibility of human-engineered organisms at the genetic level. Sounds like an obvious safety feature that should make its way into all future synthetic biology research, right? It is—until you consider how even benign innovations can change in the hands of resourceful adversaries. Such consideration doesn't fall within the parameters of the normal research process, but it's precisely what RTTA seeks to provide.

"Because the threat of the spread of such organisms is reduced in this way, it is possible that bad actors who want to create a dangerous novel bioweapon would be able to practice doing so without the risk that would normally accompany working with bacteria that could reproduce outside the lab and therefore be safer and more secure in developing that weapon," Guston wrote. "The real trick is to ask these questions as the research is going on, and not once you have the product in hand."

Guston and Sarewitz shy away from the word "prediction," preferring "anticipation." RTTA does have some very predictive elements, though it's far from prognostic. "RTTA explicitly distances itself from prediction—if reliable prediction were possible, RTTA wouldn't be necessary. RTTA is a corrective, however, to the common notion that because scientific and technological futures are not knowable in detail, nothing can be done to anticipate or prepare for them," said Sarewitz.

Guston and Sarewitz have received a fair amount of pushback from the mainstream scientific community for this idea.

"When Dan and I first generated these ideas in 2000-2001, we submitted a proposal to the National Science Foundation that contained the rudiments of this work," he said. "The reviewers were mostly quite hostile to the ideas we were espousing, indeed seeing them as hostile to the idea of free science in some instances. Over the years that we have presented this work, I have received numerous questions about whether this means that I'm hostile to basic, or to fundamental, or to curiosity-driven research, and the answer is no, that's beside the point. What we're talking about here is a coherent and self-conscious version of what goes on anyway, with a broader aspect of participation and understanding of what relevant expertise is."

To Guston, the RTTA is really just a modern version of common-sense safety precautions, like goggles, biosafety suits, or the institutional review board. "Creating risk for people outside of the laboratory is not part of the scientific ethos," he said.

Gain-of-function research remains open to a very small number of labs, as does genetically engineering new and forms of *E. coli,* or researching the genetic root of autobiographic memory, extreme height, etc. But biological knowledge is just knowledge. Today's Kickstarter project on engineering glowing plants (by injecting them with the enzyme luciferase) is tomorrow's billion-dollar blockbuster drug or bioweapon.

It may be time to start talking about science differently—at least when it comes to national security. The good news is this: if the current predicament conclusively reveals anything about the future, it's that science will survive even these attempts to better predict it.

Periodical and Internet Sources Bibliography

The following articles have been selected to supplement the diverse views presented in this chapter.

Debra Decker, "Fresh Ideas Needed to Prevent WMD Proliferation," The Stimson Center, May 31, 2016. https://www.stimson.org/content/fresh-ideas-needed-prevent-wmd-proliferation.

Bryan R. Early and Mark T. Nance, "Here's How the UN is Working to Stop Terrorists From Getting Weapons of Mass Destruction," *The Washington Post*, May 3, 2016. https://www.washingtonpost.com/news/monkey-cage/wp/2016/05/03/heres-how-the-u-n-is-working-to-stop-terrorists-from-getting-weapons-of-mass-destruction/?utm_term=.5ed0073b5802.

Dan Elliot, "Over Budget and Behind Schedule, US Plant to Destroy Chemical Weapons a Hazard to Workers," *Chicago Tribune*, March 29, 2018. https://www.chicagotribune.com/news/nationworld/ct-chemical-weapons-plant-setbacks-20180329-story.html.

Bob Graham, "How to Prevent Terrorists From Using Weapons of Mass Destruction," The Heritage Foundation, December 22, 2008. https://www.heritage.org/defense/commentary/how-prevent-terrorists-using-weapons-mass-destruction.

David Hambling, "These are Syria's Chemical Weapons. Here's How to Destroy Them," *Popular Mechanics*, April 13, 2018. https://www.popularmechanics.com/military/weapons/a19804988/how-to-destroy-syrias-chemical-weapons/.

Andrew Higgins, "Russia Destroys Chemical Weapons, and Faults US for Not Doing So," *The New York Times*, September 27, 2017. https://www.nytimes.com/2017/09/27/world/europe/russia-putin-chemical-weapons.html.

Ian Johnston, "Security Services Concerned Amateur 'Biohackers' Could Create Biological Weapons Academic Says," *Independent*, September 6, 2016. https://www.independent.co.uk/news/science/biohackers-gene-genome-editing-biological-weapons-craft-beer-hackney-a7229106.html.

Reed Karaim, "Chemical and Biological Weapons: Can They be Eliminated or Controlled," *CQ Researcher*, December 13, 2013. https://library.cqpress.com/cqresearcher/document. php?id=cqresrre2013121300.

Togzhan Kassenova, "Preventing WMD Proliferation: Myths and Realities of Strategic Trade Controls," Carnegie Endowment for International Peace, January 25, 2012. https:// carnegieendowment.org/2012/01/25/preventing-wmd-proliferation-myths-and-realities-of-strategic-trade-controls-pub-46631.

Sharon Squassoni, "Why Deterrence Failed to Prevent Syrian Use of WMD," Center for Strategic and International Studies, November 13, 2014. https://www.csis.org/analysis/why-deterrence-failed-prevent-syrian-use-wmd.

For Further Discussion

Chapter 1

1. Explain how the United States and Russia do not see eye-to-eye when it comes to chemical and biological weapons.
2. How were Britain and Germany using similar methods in the early years and discovery of chemical weapons?

Chapter 2

1. Discuss Hitler's personal experience with chemical weapons and why he elected not to use them against Allied armies in World War II but had no qualms using them against the Jewish population.
2. Explain the key differences between chemical and biological weapons.

Chapter 3

1. Discuss the variety of terrible consequences, besides death, that terrorists may want to happen to the targets of their terrorism.
2. Discuss the pros and cons from the perspective of a terrorist of using chemical, biological, or nuclear weapons.

Chapter 4

1. Discuss the challenges presented to human society by bioterrorism, most specifically its detection and response by medical staff.
2. What is the risk-benefit analysis pertaining to biological weapons, and how does the issue of scientific publication play a role?

Organizations to Contact

The editors have compiled the following list of organizations concerned with the issues debated in this book. The descriptions are derived from materials provided by the organizations. All have publications or information available for interested readers. The list was compiled on the date of publication of the present volume; the information provided here may change. Be aware that many organizations take several weeks or longer to respond to inquiries, so allow as much time as possible.

Arms Control Association
1200 18th St. NW, Ste. 1175, Washington, DC 20036
Phone: (202) 463-8270
Email: Use contact page
Website: www.armscontrol.org/

The Arms Control Association is a nonpartisan membership organization dedicated to promoting public understanding of and support for effective arms control policies.

Belfer Center for Science and International Affairs
79 John F. Kennedy St., Cambridge, MA 02138
Phone: (617) 495-9858
Email: Sharon_Wilke@hks.harvard.edu
Website: www.belfercenter.org

This university think tank specializes in research, teaching, and training in international security and diplomacy, environmental and resource issues, and science and technology policy. Belfer Center alumni trained as experts in nuclear issues have assisted the US government and through their efforts have reduced nuclear terrorism.

Centers for Disease Control and Prevention (CDC)
1600 Clifton Rd., Atlanta, GA 30329-4027
Phone: (800) 232-4636
Email: Use contact page
Website: www.cdc.gov www.cdc.gov

The Centers for Disease Control and Prevention is a governmental agency that protects Americans from health, safety, and security threats including bioterrorism. The CDC's website provides a wealth of information on bioterrorism.

Council on Foreign Relations (CFR)
58 East 68th St., New York, NY 10065
Phone: (212) 434-9400
Email: communications@cfr.org
Website: www.cfr.org

The Council on Foreign Relations is an independent, nonpartisan organization and think tank, interested in providing information so people can understand the world and the foreign policy choices facing the United States and other countries.

Department of Homeland Security (DHS)
The Honorable Kirstjen M. Nielsen, Secretary of Homeland Security, Washington, DC 20528
Phone: (202) 282-8000
Email: DHSSecretary@hq.dhs.gov
Website: www.dhs.gov

The Department of Homeland Security uses a wide variety of media and publications, all available through the website, to keep Americans updated about issues of concern.

Emerging Pathogens Institute (EPI)
2055 Mowry Rd., Gainesville, FL 32610
Phone: (352) 273-7526
Email: See contact page
Website: http://www.epi.ufl.edu/

A team of experts are at work at the Emerging Pathogens Institute studying the emergence and possible prevention of animal, plant, and human pathogens, including some of the agents often mentioned as possible biological weapons such as influenza and the ebola virus.

Heritage Foundation
214 Massachusetts Ave. NE, Washington DC 20002-4999
Phone: (202) 546-4400
Email: info@heritage.org
Website: www.heritage.org

The Heritage Foundation is a conservative research and educational institution. This organization promotes traditional American values, free enterprise, limited government, and a strong national defense.

International Committee of the Red Cross (ICRC)
19 Avenue de la paix, 1202 Geneva, Switzerland
Phone: +41 22 734 60 01
Email: Use contact page
Website: www.icrc.org/en

The ICRC is an independent, neutral organization based on the Geneva Conventions of 1949, ensuring humanitarian protection and assistance for victims of armed conflict and other situations of violence. Information on terrorism is available on its site, blog, and e-shop PDF's such as *International Humanitarian Law.*

Nuclear Threat Initiative (NTI)
1776 Eye St. NW, Ste. 600, Washington, DC 20006
Phone: (202) 296-4810
Email: contact@nti.org
Website: www.nti.org

The Nuclear Threat Initiative works to prevent attacks with weapons of mass destruction, including chemical and biological weapons. NTI works with world leaders and citizens to prevent the use of chemical bombs and to balance technology and research without the threat of biological toxins.

Organization for the Prohibition of Chemical Weapons (OPCW)
2517 JR The Hague, Netherlands
Phone: +31 70 416 3300
Email: none provided
Website: www.opcw.org

The Organization for the Prohibition of Chemical Weapons implements the Chemical Weapons Convention, which attempts to have a world that is free of the threat of chemical weapons.

Stimson Center
1211 Connecticut Ave. NW, 8th Fl., Washington, DC 20036
Phone: (202) 223-5956
Email: communications@stimson.org
Website: www.stimson.org

The Stimson Center is a nonpartisan policy research agency with a mission to promote security and prosperity, protect people and preserve the planet. The staff of experts at the Stimson Center maintains extensive articles about chemical weapons, biological weapons, and terrorism.

Bibliography of Books

Peter Bergen, *The Longest War: The Enduring Conflict Between American and al-Qaeda*. New York, NY: Free Press, 2011.

Howard Blum, *Dark Invasion: 1915: Germany's Secret War and the Hunt for the First Terrorist Cell in America*. New York, NY: Harper, 2014.

Peter Brookes, *A Devil's Triangle: Terrorism, Weapons of Mass Destruction, and Rogue States*. Lanham, MD: Rowen & Littlefield, 2005.

Jeremy K. Brown, *Warfare in the 21st Century*. New York, NY: H. W. Wilson, 2003.

Jennet Conant, *Man of the Hour: James B. Conant, Warrior Scientist*. New York, NY: Simon & Schuster, 2017.

Robert Curley, *Weapons of Mass Destruction*. New York, NY: Rosen Publishing, 2012.

Zygmunt F. Dembek, *Medical Aspects of Biological Warfare*. Fort Sam Houston, TX: United States Army Medical Department Center and School, 2007.

Kassem Eid, *My Country: A Syrian Memoir*. New York, NY: Bloomsbury Publishing, 2018.

Reese W. Erlich, *Inside Syria: The Backstory of Their Civil War and What the World Can Expect*. Amherst, NY: Prometheus Books, 2014.

Jeanne Guillemin, *Biological Weapons: From the Invention of State Sponsored Programs to Contemporary Bioterrorism*. New York, NY: Columbia University Press, 2005.

Judith Herbst, *The History of Weapons*. Minneapolis, MN: Twenty-First Century Books, 2006.

Gary Hurst, *Field Management of Chemical and Biological Casualties Handbook.* Fort Sam Houston, TX: Borden Institute, 2016.

Annie Jacobsen, *The Pentagon's Brain: An Uncensored History of DARPA, America's Top Secret Military Research Agency.* New York, NY: Little Brown & Company, 2015.

Lynn C. Klotz, *Breeding Bio Insecurity: How US Biodefense is Exporting Fear, Globalizing Risk, and Making Us All Less Secure.* Chicago, IL: University of Chicago Press, 2009.

Judith Miller, *Germs: Biological Weapons and Americ's Secret War.* New York, NY: Simon & Schuster, 2001.

Pierre Razoux, *The Iran-Iraq War.* Cambridge, MA: The Belknap Press of Harvard University Press, 2015.

Jonathan B. Tucker, *War of Nerves: Chemical Warfare from World War I to Al-Qaeda.* New York, NY: Pantheon Books, 2006.

Index

A

aerosol and spray dispersion, 26, 27, 29–30, 34, 35, 46, 98, 136, 137, 138, 166, 182

anthrax, 26–28, 33, 34, 35, 36, 38, 47, 48, 54, 61, 63, 64, 79, 98, 101, 103–104, 125, 130, 131, 135, 137

antibiotics, 39, 89, 99, 101–102, 137, 139, 153

antidotes, 39, 112, 115, 116, 133, 153

Assad, Bashar al-, 14, 16, 19–20, 22, 80, 84, 113, 168, 181

Aum Shinrikyo cult, 27, 60, 89, 95, 181

B

biological agents, 23–25, 27–28, 29–30, 32–33, 37–38, 57, 75–76, 77–78, 83, 103, 107, 120, 132, 143, 149, 151, 154, 159, 182

C

chemical agents, 21, 30, 38, 46, 47, 52, 60, 62, 70–73, 76, 82, 121, 165

chlorine, 15, 20, 76, 128

cholera, 26, 33, 136, 138

cyanide, 26, 36, 62

D

delivery systems, 24, 29–31, 32, 35, 57, 121, 149, 165

detection equipment and methods, 15, 29, 37, 91, 131, 132, 136, 142, 144, 151–152, 154, 166, 183

dual-use, concept of, 15, 33, 43–44, 45, 48, 64, 106, 107, 108, 109, 139, 143

E

Ebola, 99, 123–126, 131, 183–184

H

hemorrhagic fever, 47, 99, 139

H5N1 virus (bird flu), 107, 108, 179–180, 183

I

incapacitating chemical agents (ICAs), 70–71, 72, 142

infectious diseases, 25, 28, 33, 99–101, 125, 132, 134, 138, 149, 151, 183